Haunted Inns of New England

by Mark Jasper

Copyright © 2000 by Mark Jasper.

ISBN: 0-9653283-6-8

All Rights Reserved. No part of this book may be reprinted
in any form without express written permission from
On Cape Publications with the exception of brief quotations
for book reviews.

For additional copies or more information, please contact:

On Cape Publications,
P.O. Box 218
Yarmouth Port, MA 02675, USA.

www.oncapepublications.com
Email: haunted@oncapepublications.com
Toll Free: 1-877-662-5839

10 9 8 7 6 5 4 3 2

DEDICATION

To my wife Sharon, for all her help, love and support.

I would also like to dedicate this book to all the Innkeepers that participated. Even though we only met for a brief moment in time, my memories of you will never fade.

Acknowledgements

I would like to personally thank Barbara Woodbury at the Historical Society of Wells and Ogunquit, Maine and the Mystic Chamber of Commerce for their research and assistance. The Brick Store Museum, Kennebunk, Maine for providing the picture of Captain Fairfield. Special thanks to Charles Durang of Covered Bridge Press for making this book a better one.

TABLE OF CONTENTS

Massachusetts

1) Whispers - Sudbury, MA 1

2) Lizzie – Fall River, MA..7

3) The Ghost Cat – Salem, MA 13

Cape Cod & The Islands

4) The Red Headed Woman – Nantucket, MA....................17

5) Put That Back, It's Mine – Martha's Vineyard, MA........20

6) Help Me, Help Me – Barnstable, MA............................23

7) Mischievous Lady – Barnstable, MA............................26

8) Doctor and Sarah – Falmouth, MA..............................30

9) Forget Me Not – Falmouth, MA 34

10) Remember Me – Brewster, MA 37

11) The Vanishing Wall – Brewster, MA............................41

12) Ghost Under the Stairs – Brewster, MA.......................43

13) A Pat On the Rump – Dennis, MA 46

14) Gangsters and Ghosts – Orleans, MA..........................49

15) It's Not the Dead You Have to Worry About, ...52
It's the Living You Have to Watch Out For – Orleans, MA

16) Susan – Hyannis Port, MA 55

17) Captain, Is That You? – Sandwich, MA.........................58

18) No Bones About It – Yarmouth Port, MA 61

19) Dine with a Ghost – Yarmouth Port, MA......................64

20) The Third Floor – Centerville, MA...............................68

Rhode Island

21) Mary Poppins – Newport, RI 73

22) Footsteps – Newport, RI 77

23) House of Spirits – Newport, RI 80

Connecticut

24) Murder in the Great West Room – No. Stonington, CT ..87

25) The Ghost of John Randall – North Stonington, CT 91

26) A Woman in the Attic – North Stonington, CT 96

27) Coffin Corners – Mystic, CT 99

28) Happy Birthday – Mystic, CT 103

New Hampshire

29) Things That Go Bump In the Night – Durham, NH 111

Vermont 114

30) Mr. Darrell – Dorset, VT 115

31) A Dismembered Spirit – Dorset, VT 119

Maine

32) Haunted With Love – Ogunquit, ME 125

33) A Victorian Haunting – Ogunquit, ME 130

34) Room 2 – Ogunquit, ME................................134

35) Seven Days and Seven Nights – Kennebunk, ME........137

36) The Captain's Spell 140

    (& The In Between World) – Kennebunkport, ME 146

37) Someone Has Returned – Kennebunkport, ME..........147

38) A Wedding Story – Kennebunkport, ME 152

39) Emma's Watching – Kennebunkport, ME 156

Table of Contents

Haunted Inns of New England

INTRODUCTION

Greetings, come in, come in, I've been expecting you. I'm sorry it took so long for us to get acquainted, but tracking down haunted Inns across the New England region is quite a lengthy process. Indeed, haunted Inns are not rare but they are not common either. Once you discover one, the next task at hand is convincing the innkeeper to let you publish the story. You must gain their trust and ensure them every story will be written tastefully and accurately. After all, these are not just beautiful homes; they are places of business.

I'm certain some of you have questions to ask; by all means fire away.

• Are all of the stories true?

Yes, every story is true and has been reported without, and I do mean without, fabrication. Anything less would be unconscionable.

• Have you ever seen a ghost?

I wish I could say yes, but alas the answer is no.

• Have you sensed a presence?

Yes, for the first time I can honestly say that in one particular Inn I had such an experience. It's not something that is easily described. Simply put, you will know it if it happens to you.

• Should I be afraid?

I can say without hesitation that you will not be harmed by any of these spirits. There are no malevolent forces at work here. Besides, everyone wants to be scared just a little.

• What does a haunted Inn look like? Are the shutters falling off? Is the paint peeling? Is the grass three feet high?

You'll find these Inns to be some of the most stately and elegant places to stay in all of New England. Keep in mind, I have personally inspected every Inn and you will never meet a bigger snob. Be assured whatever Inn you chose you won't be disappointed.

• Am I guaranteed to have a ghostly encounter if I stay at one of these Inns?

No one can guarantee that, but look at it this way. Every other year my wife and I fly to Montana or Alberta, Canada, with high hopes of photographing a Grizzly Bear. To this day, I have never so much as seen a bear but just knowing that they are out there is enough for me. I hope it's enough for you.

• What made you decide to write a book on Haunted Inns?

Do you remember the winter of 1996? Well, that year my wife and I moved from Worcester, MA to Cape Cod. We moved into our new house during a horrific blizzard. Not knowing a soul in my neighborhood and being told the ground was too frozen to install cable television, I thought it was time to break out the books. That year it must have snowed every other day so driving to the bookstore became an arduous task. I began searching through boxes and uncovered a ghost book my mother bought for me years ago. It was the first ghost book I had ever read. The book was mainly about haunted houses but there was one Inn included that remained nameless. I enjoyed that story the most, simply because if I could figure out which Inn it was I could actually stay there and possibly experience something. As I read I kept thinking, I wish the author had included more Inns.

A few days after I finished the book I phoned Titcomb's Bookshop. This is how the conversation ensued. "Yes, maybe you can help me, I'm looking for a book exclusively on Haunted Inns, preferably in the New England area."

"Just a minute, I'll search on my computer. No, I'm sorry I can't find anything on Haunted Inns of New England."

"I guess I'll have to write my own book." I said with a laugh.

"Sounds like a great idea. Call us when its written we'll be happy to sell it for you."

Welcome to Haunted Inns of New England.

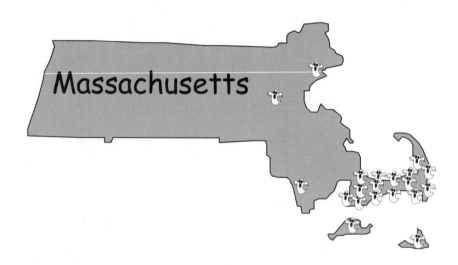

Massachusetts

WHISPERS

On a bright June morning I departed Cape Cod and journeyed up to the central part of the state. As I turned off route 20 onto Wayside Inn Road, (Sudbury, MA), the scenery quickly changed from car dealerships and fast food restaurants to rolling green pastures and dense woodlands. I soon began to spot cars parked along the narrow road and gazed upon the Inn's beautiful gristmill. A bit further up, I slowed down and meandered into the parking lot of Longfellow's Wayside Inn, made famous by Henry Wadsworth Longfellow, who wrote *Tales of a Wayside Inn* published in 1863.

When I arrived I wished I had a little more time to poke around, but I was a few minutes late and hurriedly made my way to the front desk. "Is Lee Swanson here?" I asked. The desk clerk said he would be down shortly. As I patiently waited by the gift shop, I observed and listened intently. The Wayside Inn is a bit larger than the majority of my other Inns, catering over 1000 functions a year. I was curious to see how they dealt with large numbers of businessmen and tourists streaming in for a tour or

a bite to eat. I have been to many large Inns where personal touches have all but been forgotten. I am pleased to report the Wayside Inn is not among them. The staff and management deserve high marks for their efforts. Every guest was promptly greeted and treated with kindness. In fact you almost feel as if you're in a cozy Bed and Breakfast, something very rare in my opinion.

As I was about to be overwhelmed by sinful aromas emanating from the Inn's dining room, I was introduced to Lee Swanson, Historic Coordinator. Lee is a colorful and articulate man. He's often seen at the front door dressed in Colonial attire greeting guests or giving informative talks. I had the good fortune of spending the better half of the day with Lee, touring the grounds and getting a lesson in history.

The setting, while lively with people coming and going, still manages to maintain a feeling of peace and tranquility. The old gristmill is a wonderful place for children and adults alike. It's not to be missed.

The Inn itself is truly breathtaking, originally constructed by David How in 1702. It was initially built as a two-room dwelling. Over the next 159 years, seven additions were added by the How family. In 1716 a license was granted to operate as a house of entertainment. This meant they were allowed to entertain strangers, serve food and drink and provide lodging for man and beast The 'e' was added to the name Howe after 1800.

The property remained under the control of the Howe innkeepers until 1861. Whereupon it closed and was operated as a boarding house and function hall until 1897, when E. R. Lemon purchased the estate and reopened it as an Inn. In 1923, the Inn was acquired by Henry Ford. Today it is owned by the Wayside Inn Trust/Corporation and operated as a nonprofit educational, charitable trust.

The Inn has managed to maintain its 18th Century atmosphere. Uneven wide pine floors seem to creak with every step. Original antiques found throughout the Inn include old pewter, china and handcrafted furniture. The Inn has ten spacious guestrooms; all are comfortable and uniquely decorated.

I was informed that back in the 1800s, a woman named

Jerusha Howe lived on the second floor of the home, now rooms 9 and 10. She was officially known as the Belle of Sudbury, celebrated for owning and playing the first pianoforte in Sudbury. On occasion, she would greet guests and entertain them in the parlor by performing on the pianoforte. In later years, Jerusha became somewhat of a recluse and died in her 40s. It was said that she had an English lover, who after a voyage at sea, never returned. It is Jerusha's spirit that is thought to haunt the Wayside Inn.

After climbing the steep, narrow staircase, I began to explore rooms nine and ten. I spent quite a bit of time looking for trap doors and sifting through SDS letters. What does SDS stand for? I must admit before I came to the Wayside, I had no idea, myself. SDS stands for Secret Drawer Society. Almost every room in the Inn has furniture with secret compartments. Guests leave notes for other guests to read; some even hide bits of treasure, leaving maps and clues as to their whereabouts. The tradition was started back in the early 1900s and continues to this day. The SDS is really more than just leaving notes on bits of paper. It's about sharing memories. I spent over an hour examining notes written by newlyweds, grandparents, small children and people from all over the world. It was hard not to become emotional as people I'd never met suddenly came to life, sharing their joy and wonderful memories about their stay. The more I read the more I was overcome by feelings of intense warmth, especially in room nine. It is a feeling that has never left me. I will share with you some of the more interesting notes at the end of the story.

As I mentioned earlier, Jerusha's spirit is thought to be responsible for some of the bizarre events that have been recorded over the years. Lee informed me that rooms nine and ten are the center of the Inn's ghostly activity. Although other incidents have occurred in the original parlor and newer guestrooms rebuilt in the 1950s. Some of the stories include guests, mostly men, being awakened in the early morning hours by a woman's voice whispering in their ear. Others have been known to smell a strong citrus-based perfume. It has been documented that Jerusha's favorite perfume was, in fact, citrus based.

Some guests sense a presence in rooms nine and ten and

refuse to enter altogether. Shirley, who works at the front desk, swears she heard footsteps one morning while she was completely alone in the Inn.

One guest claimed that she was visited by an apparition of a woman in room nine. The guest drew a portrait of what the woman looked like. The drawing was saved and is now stored in the Inn's Archives department.

A chambermaid while working in the newer section of the Inn reported seeing a shimmering blue figure about four feet tall in the hallway. When she looked directly at it, the figure vanished. Lee associated this sighting with a person named Ponto who was part Black, part Indian. He was purchased as a slave by a member of the How family in the 1700s and stood approximately four feet tall.

I will conclude as promised by sharing with you some of the more interesting SDS letters I uncovered. The exception is the last one, sent to me by a CPA from Virginia.

11/18/89 6:15 PM

What was that noise??? Why did the lights go out??? The sound of drums, fife, cannons and we thought that we were in the middle of a re-make of a Revolutionary War movie.

We heard that room #9 was haunted, but only now do we believe it. It only lasted about two minutes, but after checking with the front desk, they knew nothing about drums, light?

S-D-S some of the voices you hear at night, maybe ghosts....

10/20/94

I did feel a presence in this room (a good one!) She makes you feel welcome here.

12/6,7,8/94

The ghosts are real. We were each visited by her as we slept.

7/11/95

I have enjoyed this place if you are a little kid you will be scared. So you might want to sleep close to your Mom and Dad. Banging walls creeking floors and scarey doors. I was scared you probably be scared to.

P.S. There is a ghost named Jarushie, you might hear her or see her.

4/30/98

During the period of April 19 – 21, 1998, I attended a business meeting which was held at the Longfellow's Wayside Inn located in Sudbury, Mass. I registered as a guest and stayed in room number 2, on the second floor. On Sunday the 19th, I had dinner and retired to my room around 11PM. Shortly thereafter, I went to bed.

At 4:50 AM, I was awakened by what felt like fingernails scratching at the bottom of my right foot. It was a one-time scratch which started at the bottom of my foot and continued in the direction of my toes. I immediately woke up and found myself lying on my left side with my legs slightly bent. At the same instant, I felt pressure against my back, as if someone had curled up against my back and inserted their knees under mine. I attempted to roll over but couldn't because of the tremendous pressure that was holding me in place. I tried to speak, but found my jaw was in a frozen stage. I felt as though someone was right up against my back trembling uncontrollably. I then clearly heard a young women's voice whisper in my ear ---"I am very cold... you are very seductive...(followed by garbled words)...Peter."

Almost immediately, I felt release of the grasp that I was under and was able to roll over. The room was dark and I did not see anyone present. I then turned the lights on and searched the room but found no one. My doors and windows were locked from the inside.

The next morning, I related my experience to the Inn's receptionist. I then learned that a couple in a different area of the hotel had also experienced an encounter.

I stayed in the same room during the next two nights without any further encounters. I have never had any prior experiences such as this in my life. I later found out from the Inn's personnel that Jerusha Howe has been haunting the Inn for some time. No one seemed to associate the name Peter to the Jerusha stories.

Longfellow's Wayside Inn
Sudbury, Massachusetts
978-443-1776
800-339-1776

LIZZIE

Are you ready to enter the world of Lizzie Borden? What's that you say, you're a bit squeamish, axe murderers and bloody corpses are not your cup of tea? If you turn back now you'll be making a big mistake. A trip to the Lizzie Borden Bed & Breakfast (Fall River, MA) is a trip you will remember for the rest of your life. After all, not everyone can say they have toured the most infamous crime scene of the 19th century.

I must admit that before I visited this historic landmark, officially known as the Lizzie Borden Bed and Breakfast Museum, I knew very little about the case. I am certain you have all heard the famous little ditty "Lizzie Borden took an axe and gave her mother forty whacks. When she saw what she had done she gave her father forty-one." Well that little ditty is not very accurate, but we will discuss the facts of the case shortly.

First and foremost some praise is in order. Owner Martha McGinn, her staff of tour guides and historians are truly a remarkable group. They are dedicated to their cause and perform their duties with unsurpassed professionalism. I thoroughly enjoyed myself as my private tour guide bombarded me with facts about the case. After my private tour I joined one of the public tours given 11:00 a.m. to 3:00 p.m. It was quite a treat watching people's expressions as they viewed gruesome crime scene photos and examined old newspaper clippings.

Looking for more than a tour? You're welcome to spend the night. In 1996, this 1845 Greek Revival was transformed from a private residence into a functional Bed and Breakfast. For breakfast, guests will be served a similar meal to the one the Bordens ate on the morning of the murders, which included bananas, johnnycakes, sugar cookies and coffee. The three-day-old mutton broth has been excluded.

The entire house has been impeccably restored with no stone left unturned. The décor is distinctly Victorian. Beautiful antique furniture is found throughout the house accompanied by lovely wall coverings. The three guestrooms and two spacious suites are located on the second and third floors. When the Bordens owned the house, the first room on the second floor was considered the guestroom, now called the John Morse Guest Room. This room is where Lizzie's stepmother was found murdered. A copy of the original photograph of her body lying beside the bed hangs on the wall. You'll have to remember to book early if you want to sleep in this room; it is by far the most sought after.

Interesting artifacts are found throughout the house including one of Lizzie's dresses and various hatchets. Which hatchet was the murder weapon remains unknown. In the library there is a wealth of information about the case for guests to sort through. Old books, videos and newspapers articles are always on display.

For the adventurous, the Inn has put together special Halloween and Murder Anniversary packages. Wait till you see what the Inn has planned for you on those particular dates.

For those of you interested in case facts, here they are, courtesy of the Lizzie Borden Museum:

Who's Who:

Andrew J. Borden – Lizzie's Father –Found dead on sofa in first floor sitting room. Had been napping after reading the Providence Journal. He died more than hour after Abby.

Abby Borden – Lizzie's stepmother – Found dead in second floor guest bedroom. Had been changing pillow shams. Died more than one hour before Andrew.

Lizzie Borden – Says she was in the house when Abby was killed, in barn out back when Andrew was killed.

Bridget Sullivan – Family maid – Says she was outside washing windows when Abby was killed, in her third floor bedroom when Andrew was killed.

Emma Borden- Lizzie's Older Sister- Visiting friends in Fairhaven, Mass.

John V. Morse – Lizzie's and Emma's Uncle- Had stayed the previous night in the guest bedroom where Abby was killed. Was visiting relatives in Fall River the day of the murders. Some think his alibi was too good.

Chronology
Aug. 4, 1892 Andrew & Abby Borden murdered
Aug. 11, 1892 Lizzie Borden arrested
June 5, 1893 Trial begins

June 20, 1893 Lizzie Borden acquitted

June 1, 1927 Lizzie Borden dies at age 66, leaves $30,000 to the Fall River Animal Rescue League

June 10, 1927 Emma Borden, Lizzie's sister, dies at age 76

Not Quite Right

The little ditty that immortalized the crime is not quite accurate.

• Abby Borden was Andrew Borden's second wife and Lizzie Borden's stepmother, not mother.

• Most authorities believe a hatchet, not an axe, did in the Borden's, though the murder weapon was never found.

• Abby Borden received 19 blows, not 40.

• Andrew Borden received 10 blows, not 41.

For more information about the case, contact Archivist Bill Pavao. Bill will be more than happy to share his knowledge with you.

By now you are probably wondering, do things go bump in the night here? Michelle, my personal tour guide, believes the house is, as she puts it, occupied. Exactly what does occupied mean? It means that spirits are thought to reside here. Thankfully, they are of good nature. Nothing evil has ever

happened here. They range from little mischievous pranks to incidents that are certain to make your heart pound. Michelle's mother, who used to be the cook, reported the first sign of activity. She had just begun preparing for the function that was to be held at the house, when she said she distinctly heard the sound of a wooden screen door closing. This seemed impossible, simply because at the time, there was no wooden screen door on the house. She also heard the sound of people walking and furniture being moved on the second floor. This happened when the second floor was vacant.

Michelle also remembers hearing some unexplainable voices on the second floor. After the contractors had finished working on the second floor in the room called the Andrew and Abby suite, Michelle decided the room needed to be cleaned. While she was working, the sound of two women speaking could be heard emanating from the John Morse Guest Room. She dropped what she was doing and walked toward the room. As soon as she opened the door the voices abruptly stopped.

The next incident took place about a month and a half after the Bed and Breakfast had opened for business. Housekeeping had just finished cleaning the rooms and making the beds. One of the housekeepers walked back into the John Morse Guest Room and suddenly fled down the stairs, ran through the gift shop and out of the Inn, never to return. The housekeeper said when she entered the room, she walked over to the commode stand to put the sheets away. When she turned around she saw the imprint of a body on the bed.

Guests have also reported strange happenings. Some have reported hearing a woman sobbing on the third floor, while others have seen an apparition of an older woman with gray hair wearing dark Victorian clothing. She is usually seen doing various chores, such as dusting or pulling up the blankets on the bed. A woman sleeping on the third floor felt as if someone was pressing on her chest.

The Inn is home to several black cats. A few guests have reported hearing the cats meowing in the middle of the night. Some have even felt the cats walking on them. What's so strange about that, you ask? The black cats found throughout the house are of the stuffed animal variety; in other words, they're not real.

I hope you have enjoyed your brief tour of the Lizzie Borden Bed and Breakfast Museum. If you decide to visit, you'll meet people from across the world as they try to solve one of the greatest murder mysteries of the 19th Century.

The Lizzie Borden Bed & Breakfast Museum
Fall River, Massachusetts
508-675-7333

THE GHOST CAT

They said it couldn't be done. "I don't know of any haunted Inns in Salem," said one Innkeeper. "Forget it, there aren't any around here," said another. How can this be, I thought to myself, of all the places in New England. Not to worry, I don't give up that easily. After a relentless search I am pleased to report that I have uncovered the only haunted Inn in Salem, known as the Stephen Daniels House. (Salem, MA)

Finding this little gem was no easy task. Salem is a maze of crowded shops and busy streets. I must have gotten lost at least five times before I found the narrow side street where the Inn is located.

Let's go in, shall we, or at least try. On occasion busy innkeepers do forget about their appointments. There's nothing more disappointing than grasping the door handle only to find it locked, or hearing an assistant say, "No, the innkeeper isn't here, did you have an appointment?" I'm going to hold my breath while I knock on the door. "Hello, are you Kay?" "Yes, won't you come in." It looks like I'm going to get my story.

The Stephen Daniels House had its beginnings in the year of 1667, originally built by a prominent sea captain known as Stephen Daniels. In 1756 his great grandson added a large front parlor and more bedrooms.

The Daniels family retained ownership of the home until 1931. It remained unoccupied until 1945 when a family from Oregon transformed the home into a tearoom and four-bedroom guesthouse. After 18 years of ownership the house was sold to the present owner, Chicago native Kay Gill.

Kay has a wonderfully distinct personality. Most innkeepers will often ask if they will receive a copy of the book after its published. Kay said and I quote "Do me a favor, don't send me a copy of the book." After that comment I laughed so hard my ribs ached. Kay is really a very warm person with a great sense of humor. Simply put, she's someone you will remember for the rest of your life.

Spending a night in the Stephen Daniels House is like sleeping in your favorite antique shop. The entire Inn is adorned with 18th and 19th century antiques. In the dining room along the side of the enormous harvest table are rare Punch and Judy puppets and Canton porcelain. Walk up the back stairway and you'll discover Kay's collection of well preserved antique wooden ducks.

The Inn's four guestrooms are furnished with authentic Colonial furniture and beautiful hand painted portraits. Other features include spacious common rooms decorated to perfection, and romantic fireplaces.

The Stephen Daniels House is the oldest Inn in Salem and ghostly apparitions have been reported. One gentleman claimed he saw an apparition of a man standing in the dining room that was identical to a portrait on the wall. Another woman said she witnessed an apparition of a woman fall and come crashing down the staircase.

Of course the main attraction of the Inn is the ghost of a gray and black stripped tiger cat. Guests have often seen this ghost cat, as it darts in and out of rooms and leaps onto beds. One woman reported feeling a cat around her neck while she slept. Some repeat guests have even been known to leave saucers of milk beside their bed.

Obviously this cat must have belonged to the Daniels family but why it haunts the Inn remains a mystery. Sometime before Kay bought the Inn she painted a portrait of a gray tiger cat, which now hangs in a guestroom on the second floor. Incredibly, the painting is the spitting image of the ghostly cat that haunts the Stephen Daniels House.

Stephen Daniels House
Salem, Massachusetts
978-744-5709

Cape Cod & the Islands

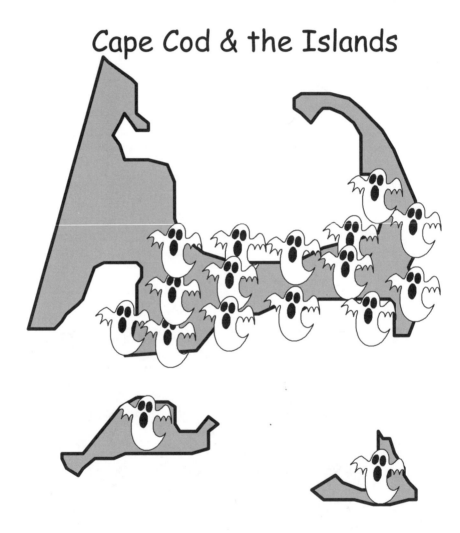

THE RED HEADED WOMAN

The morning I boarded the ferry from Hyannis to Nantucket the weather was less than ideal. You would expect the end of June to be warm and wonderful. Instead, it was misty and gray with fog so intensely thick you could barely see the person in front of you. That being said, it didn't seem to put a damper on the hordes of tourists traveling with me that morning. As we docked, people swarmed to the exits carrying camera lenses as big as bazookas, for what I have no idea. As I took my place in line, I slowly crept down the steps and onto Straight Wharf. With a small knapsack in hand I scurried past hundreds of tourists when the unthinkable happened. I was carrying my knapsack upside down. Everything inside including my tape recorder fell out with a thunderous crash. Tapes going in one direction, plastic carrying cases in another, as a crowd of onlookers gasped. Pretending as if this is how I normally test my equipment for durability, I quickly gathered my belongings before they were trampled and dashed out of sight.

I will not attempt to describe the Island itself. Nantucket is a place you must simply experience for yourself.

The Inn we will be visiting today is the Sherburne Inn. Stay close behind as we head from Straight Wharf to Main Street then onto South Water, up Broad Street, cross Center Street and finally arrive at 10 Gay Street.

The Sherburne Inn was constructed in 1835. At the time it was headquarters for the Atlantic Silk Company, owned by William H. Gardner, Samuel B. Tuck and William Coffin. The company possessed one of only two power looms in the world. Hard times hit the silk factory and by 1844 it was no longer in operation. In the mid 1800s the factory was divided into two separate units. The east side was converted into a guesthouse, now the Sherburne Inn.

Over time the Inn has changed hands quite a few times and is now owned and being meticulously maintained by Susan Gasparich and Dale Hamilton. This magnificent Greek Revival has been restored with exquisite taste. The two lavishly decorated front parlors with Victorian accent pieces are wonderful rooms for conversation. The English wall coverings are a blend of soft prints and regal colors. Eight guestrooms are highlighted with canopy or four poster beds, all king or queen sized. Plush hand woven oriental rugs compliment the antique hardwood floors and enrich the Inn's character.

When Susan and Dale purchased the Inn in March of 1994, they were informed by the previous owners the Inn was haunted. They said a former owner had reported seeing a woman dressed in Victorian garb, wearing a white dress, with long red hair. Dale and Susan commented that shortly after they became innkeepers, bizarre events began to occur.

A guest staying in one of the rooms told Susan that at approximately 2:00 in the morning she was awakened by what she described as a passage of someone. She described seeing a misty cloud-like figure float by. In the morning she said to her husband, "I must have had a dream last night." While she was describing her experience to him, he said he awoke at 2:00 in the morning and saw the very same cloud-like image. Apparently neither of them knew the other was awake.

A gentleman staying in a different room said he was in the bathroom about to shower when he noticed an old-fashioned lock on the door. He clearly remembers the old latch being in the unlocked position before he stepped into the shower. When he came out the latch had been thrown into the locked position. One guest, after being locked out on the balcony of his room, had to yell for someone to let him in.

Susan thinks the ghost is a bit of a trickster but quite harmless. The strange presence that is often felt by her and guests is one of peace and tranquility, certainly nothing of a malevolent nature. Although one time a couple staying in room number five told Susan of a rather hair-raising experience they had endured one evening. In the middle of the night the couple awoke to a strange and frightening noise. The sound of long fingernails starting at the top of the wall and slowly scratching their way down echoed in their room. Then it would start again, fingernails slowly scratching from top to bottom. The couple did not investigate.

Who this ghost is, most certainly is anyone's guess. Dale and Susan speculate there might be a connection to the silk factory, but no one is really certain.

Sherburne Inn
Nantucket Island, Massachusetts
508-228-4425

Put That Back, It's Mine!

Fasten your seatbelt, you're about to embark on a motion odyssey ride to Martha's Vineyard via the Edgartown Ferry. It's an exhilarating ride from Falmouth harbor, taking about an hour. At times you'll feel like you're traveling at warp speed, darting around buoys and slicing through waves. If you're not wearing a wet suit it's best to sit inside; the slightest chop sends water catapulting over the bow, drenching the unsuspecting tourist. All and all, it's great fun and conveniently drops you off in Edgartown Harbor, one of the most picturesque harbors on earth.

I have often been asked, "Do you have a favorite Inn?" or "What town do you like best?" I will respond to the first question by saying every Inn I have included in this book I hold near and dear to my heart. The simple truth is I really have no favorite. On the other hand, I do have a favorite town and it happens to be the one I am currently writing about.

Edgartown is rejuvenation for the soul, a poetic dream, if you will. I could think of nothing more enjoyable than strolling its narrow flower laden streets or gazing upon its gracious sea captains' homes. Edgartown has been discovered but it still remains an unspoiled gem, glistening by the sea.

Just a short jaunt from Edgartown Harbor, beyond the quaint shops, brings us to a classic 19th Century Inn known as the Bailey House.

I'm not certain which was more memorable, the historic Inn itself or the delightful staff that seems to go above and beyond. While I was waiting in the lovely courtyard for Innkeeper Sarah Grady to arrive, I was repeatedly asked, "Can I get you a cold drink? Are you sure? Just let me know if you change your mind." I would like to say to the staff, your professionalism and kindness did not go unnoticed.

The Bailey House is an interesting blend of historic and contemporary flavors. The front sitting room is a mix of unusual antiques and comfortable contemporary furnishings. The fourteen guestrooms are all bright and cheerful and have a more traditional flair. The flower filled courtyards are wonderful for relaxing, as is the inviting front porch. A perfect spot to curl up with a good book, or fall asleep under the stars.

Sarah Grady has been the Bailey House Innkeeper for the past four and a half years. She's a joy to be with and always wears a smile. Sarah informed me that the house first became an Inn 17 years ago. During renovations workers found old newspapers dating back to the 1790s, children's marbles and six very old little girls shoes, all made of leather. Sarah and her staff believe the Inn may be haunted by the spirit of a playful little girl. Sarah mentioned that one time a couple staying in room 3 reported hearing someone walking up and down the stairs all night. At the time, the Inn was completely empty. Room 3 in particular seems to be the center of the Inn's ghostly activity. While doing some renovations in that very room, a startled painter dropped his paintbrush and took three steps toward the hall. He called out to Sarah who he thought was playing a trick on him. Sarah came walking out of another guestroom. "You weren't just over there?" he exclaimed. The painter reported seeing a dark shadow float across the hallway and disappear. Sarah stated that other people including herself have witnessed this dark figureless shadow floating across room 3, particularly in winter. Some guests have even seen shadow-like feet under their door.

Chambermaids have also reported neatly putting things away only to come back and find everything rearranged.

During the interview, we were joined by one of the Inn's employees Karen Anderson. Karen told me about some things that had happened to her two days before my arrival. During a routine cleaning of room 3, Karen discovered an antique hairpin in a side drawer next to the bed. She found it quite ironic since she had just finished reading the night before about another haunted Inn on the Island and their experience with old hair pins.

Karen removed the hairpin from the drawer and carried it upstairs to room 7, which was next on her list to clean. Before she started she wanted to show Sarah the unusual hairpin she had found. The moment Karen stepped out of room 7, the hairpin was suddenly plucked from her hand and mysteriously vanished. Karen said, "it felt like someone just knocked it out of my hand." Thinking it must have landed somewhere on the floor she began an endless search. The hairpin was no where to be found. At that point she walked downstairs and began searching room 3. Karen decided to check the bedside drawer where she had originally found the object. As she slowly pulled open the drawer she found herself staring at the little antique hairpin.

It was almost as if an angry little girl spoke to Karen and said, "Put that back, it's mine!"

Author's note: Shortly before this book went to publication, the owners of this Inn became a little nervous, well very nervous, about using the Inn's real name. They requested that I change the name of the Inn as well as the names of the employees.

You'll have to find this one on your own!

HELP ME! HELP ME!

If you are a history buff, you will adore the Crocker Tavern bed and breakfast. It is located on historic 6A in the village of Barnstable, MA. The house had its beginnings in 1734. By 1754 a wealthy tailor named Cornielius Crocker converted the home into a tavern. It served as a stagecoach stop and food and lodging establishment well into the 1800s. The Whig party used the tavern as one of their main meeting places during the Revolutionary War. Supposedly, a representative to the King was once killed in a sword fight in the front parlor. They say there is even a notch on the beam from the sword fight that is still visible if you look carefully.

In 1926 the two remaining Crocker women, now since passed away, bequeathed the house to the society for Preservation of New England Antiquities. It was then operated as a house museum by the society during the 1970s. It was then sold with preservation restrictions to a private owner and then resold a couple times during the 1980s.

In 1993 Sue and Jeff Carlson purchased the property, turning it into a functional Inn for the first time since the 1800s.

This Federal style colonial has five charming rooms complete with authentic period furnishings and a lovely parlor for relaxing. I was told most of the Inn looks the way it did back in the 1700 and 1800s, right down to the original wood work and horsehair plaster.

After a most interesting discussion about the Inn's history, we began to discuss some of the ghostly activity that has occurred periodically over the years. Sue told me I should start by speaking to the owner of the famous Jacks Out Back restaurant in Yarmouthport, MA. Sue said he had a most unusual experience one night while house-sitting, back when the historical society owned the house.

I met with Jack Smith one afternoon at his restaurant. It is always jam-packed with locals and tourists alike, so I arrived at closing time. While, Jack was cleaning up I listened as he told of his experience. Jack said it was probably about 17 years ago. He was house sitting for about 3 weeks during the winter for the historical society. One night while residing in a room on the second floor, Jack began to hear heavy footsteps coming up the stairs. Terrified, he flew out of bed dressed only in a pair of shorts. He was the only one in the house at the time, so he came to the conclusion that someone must have broken in. Jack stood almost frozen in his room as he listened to the heavy footsteps climb the stairs, turn right and walk down the hall. He could feel the vibrations as the footsteps drew near. Suddenly, they stopped directly outside his door. Heart pounding, Jack slowly opened the door only to find he was staring into darkness. Jack said "I don't know what it was, but someone or something was definitely there."

Now we'll continue our chat with the Carlsons. They have some most interesting stories of their own, that I think you will enjoy.

Sue told of a guest that recently had a bit of a run-in with their resident ghost. "A couple were staying on the second floor in a room known as the James Otis room. In the middle of the night, the woman awoke to find a human figure walking across the room toward her. At first she thought it was her husband until she reached over and discovered he was lying beside her. As the figure moved closer and closer she found herself staring face to face with a ghostly apparition of a woman. As soon as she tried to wake her husband, the ghost suddenly vanished."

Another guest, who was a self-proclaimed witch from California, was staying in a room named Aunt Lydia's room. In the dead of the night she claimed the bed started shaking violently. Being from California, she thought it was an earthquake. When she found out that there was no earthquake she became so unnerved she immediately requested to be moved to another room. The Carlsons said another woman staying in that same room told of the bed shaking violently in the middle of the night as well.

In my opinion, the strangest experience of all happened to owner Jeff Carlson. Jeff said on two separate occasions in the middle of the night, when Sue was fast asleep, he heard a voice. Jeff said, "I remember it clearly. It was very eerie sounding and definitely the voice of a woman." The ghostly voice from out of the darkness repeated the same words over and over, "Help Me! Help Me!"

Author's note: The Carlson's believe the ghost may possibly be one of the Crocker women that passed away years ago.

Crocker Tavern Bed & Breakfast
Barnstable, Massachusetts
508-362-5115

THE MISCHIEVOUS LADY

This Victorian beauty known as the Beechwood Inn is located on historic 6A in Barnstable, MA.

Upon arrival, I was promptly greeted by two of the Inn's residents, a pair of overly friendly golden retrievers. As I opened the door of my car, one of the goldens dropped a sticky tennis ball in my lap. After a quick game of fetch, I made my way to the back porch where I first met Ken, the proud owner of the Inn.

Ken and Debbie Traugot purchased the Inn in 1994. The house was originally constructed in 1853 by a gentleman in the hat business. It remained a private residence until 1980 when it was converted into a charming Victorian Inn.

The Beechwood is considered a Queen Anne Victorian Inn with Greek Revival features. It is adorned with magnificent antiques emphasizing Eastlike, cottage and Victorian styles. The Inn features six guestrooms, an elegant living room, and a private dining room.

After a wonderful tour of the Inn we sat down and began to discuss their resident ghost. Ken stated that when they first

bought the Inn they worked very closely with the former owner for about a month, learning the tricks of the trade. After becoming good friends, Ken and Debbie were having dinner with the former owners and a few other couples who were frequent guests of the Inn. As the Traugots listened, an intriguing conversation began to unfold. The former owners started to converse about their resident ghost named Arthur. They said Arthur was probably just a figment of their imagination and not to worry. Ken and Debbie just looked at each other and thought, maybe Arthur was to blame for some of the strange and unexplainable occurrences that were happening in their Inn.

When the Traugots first purchased the Inn, the ghost began playing little mischievous tricks and games. For instance, Ken would walk into a room, turn on the lights and often find a bulb out in one of the chandeliers or light fixtures. He'd race to the back room, grab a ladder and a new bulb, only to find the old bulb had merely been loosened. This was a fairly common occurrence, driving Ken crazy at times. Other interesting things that have happened include large power tools being mysteriously moved from one side of a room to another when absolutely no one was around and a motorized skylight that has been known to open and close by itself, as if some unknown force had pushed the button.

As time went on events became more startling. The Traugots will certainly never forget their first Christmas in the Inn. They had placed candles in each of the guest-rooms, as most people do around Christmas time. On one particular night they were turning off the candles in the unoccupied guest-rooms. Suddenly, a strange presence had fallen upon them, seemingly following them from room to room. Ken said, "I can't explain it, but someone was definitely there and for some peculiar reason it felt very much like a female presence."

Another strange event that occurred took place in a room they call the Rose room. A mother and daughter had been staying in the room for a couple of days. When they checked out they returned the key, said their good-byes and left. Soon after, one of their cleaning assistants attempted to enter the room. She put the key in the door, turned the lock but the door would not open. She attempted to unlock the door several more times but still no luck. Finally, out of frustration, she located Ken and told him of her trouble with the door. He immediately took the key and tried the lock himself. Once again the key turned perfectly in the lock, but strangely the door would not open. Astounded, Ken walked around and peered into the room through a window. Apparently, there is another lock on the inside of the door. A heavy old dead bolt latch that had been thrown into a fully locked position. Ken could not believe his eyes. The only way a person could lock the door from the inside and still manage to escape would be to open the window, pry the screen off and climb out, not an easy task. "We certainly didn't see the mother and daughter climbing out of windows. It's just impossible," exclaimed Ken.

The Traugots feel their ghost is friendly, but can be a bit mischievous at times. They also feel the ghost is a woman and makes her presence known more often in the dead of winter and middle of summer. On occasion when the second floor of the Inn is empty, eerie footsteps can be heard as if someone is trying to say, "You're not alone."

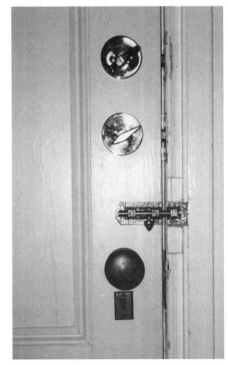

"So who is this woman that resides in the Beechwood Inn?" I asked. Ken replied, "We really have no idea, we haven't even named her yet. We're hoping some day she tells us who she really is."

A few months after the interview, I received this note from Ken:

Two women were visiting and staying in the Lilac room. A few times one of the women would leave in their car, but not the other. Debbie entered the room to do some cleaning and walked in on one of the women. After excusing herself, she planned on coming back later.

Debbie heard the two women leave and double checked by peeking out the window as they got into their car. She went into the Lilac room only to hear a female voice say "Good Morning." Thinking she had made a mistake again, she backed out of the room. Knowing she just saw that both women had left, she re-entered the room, looked around and found no one!

Beechwood Inn
Barnstable, Massachusetts
508-362-6618

The Mischievous Lady   **29**

THE DOCTOR AND SARAH

Charming, warm and elegant are a few words I would use to describe the Village Green Inn, Falmouth, MA. If asked to describe the innkeepers, Diane and Don Crosby, the same words would certainly come to mind.

The Crosbys purchased this 1804 Victorian style home in 1995 from former Innkeepers Linda and Donald Long. The Inn boasts five richly decorated guestrooms, a lovely dining room and a soft elegant front parlor that I found absolutely enchanting.

Guests will enjoy the Inn's spacious open porches decorated with white wicker furniture. The night I visited with the Crosbys, I was informed the former Innkeepers Linda and Donald Long would be joining us as well. I was told they have some interesting stories of their own to tell.

We all met in the back part of the Inn, which happens to be the Crosbys' living quarters. After a cold glass of lemonade, the ghost stories began to unfold. I had a hunch it was going to be a great evening.

Linda said the first time they suspected they had a ghost in the Inn came from a guest staying in one of the upstairs bedrooms, now known as the Dimmick room. As the woman was checking out she politely asked Linda if anybody had ever reported any strange happenings in the guestroom she had been staying in. Linda asked her to clarify what she meant. The woman said she was visited by an apparition of a young woman in her late teens or early twenties. She described her as having long, flowing dark hair and dressed in a white old-fashioned nightgown. The woman said the apparition hovered above her bed and appeared to have a puzzled look on her face.

After hearing this story, Linda became intrigued. She began doing quite a bit of research on the history of the house. She uncovered that only three other families had previously owned the house. The original owners, the Dimmicks, had a daughter, named Sarah who was born in 1803 and died in 1823. Unfortunately, that was all the information she found.

Linda spoke of some other strange occurrences that have happened as well. She said one time a chambermaid from Australia had been working there for the summer. Linda had a strange feeling the girl had a type of sixth sense. One day Linda asked her if she ever felt a presence on the second floor. The girl said she kept getting a feeling that she had to take very special care of the house. She also mentioned that while in the Dimmick room, a rocking chair mysteriously began rocking by itself.

Linda remembers a time when her friend and fourteen year

The Doctor and Sarah 31

old daughter were touring the Inn, when out of nowhere, the daughter said, "Mom, I'm going to wait in the car," and off she went. Weeks later, Linda asked her friend what happened. Her friend said, "I'm not supposed to tell you, but my daughter saw an apparition of a man and woman in old colonial clothes standing at the top of the stairs. The woman had on a small hat and the man was wearing some type of military uniform. She became so frightened she refused to go upstairs and headed straight for the car." Linda said her friend's daughter was so shaken, she refused to enter the Inn ever again.

Now we will hear from the present owners, Diane and Don Crosby. Diane stated that after they purchased the Inn back in 1995, the Longs shared some of their ghostly tales with them. Diane said I thought they were just stories and I really didn't pay much attention to them. Shortly after the Crosbys had settled in, Diane had a couple of experiences of her own she will never forget.

Diane said, "I think it was in November of 1995, we only had two rooms occupied at the time, one guest was out, and the other was in his room. I remember setting the breakfast table for the next morning in the dining room. All of a sudden I looked up and saw a short older man walking into the front parlor." Diane said the man had gray hair, was dressed in a plaid flannel shirt and walked with stooped shoulders. Diane was stunned; she knew one guest was out and the other one was an unusually tall man. She called out to her husband, Don, who was in the cellar. He came running up. After explaining what she had just seen, they both walked into the parlor. No one was there. At the time, it had been snowing, but not a footprint was to be found. Don had mentioned this mysterious sighting to a man that lived in town. "You've just described Doctor Tripp," the man exclaimed.

Doctor Edwin P. Tripp had bought the house in 1913. It was his place of residence, as well as his medical office. He had died a few months before Diane's sighting.

Diane remembers another time a friend had asked her if she had any more unusual sightings. She replied, "No, that was the only one." Shortly after their conversation, some guests had just arrived. As soon as Diane greeted them at the door she began to smell something burning. The smell was coming from the front parlor. One of the guests said, "It is coming from the lamp." Upon inspection, Diane found wax had been melted all over the light bulb. She was absolutely astounded, "Where did the wax come from?" she stated. Strangely, there were no candles lit in the room at the time. Diane said, "I think Doctor Tripp was just letting me know he is still around. After all, the front parlor used to be his examining room."

The Crosby's hired a chambermaid from Canada one summer who was very much into the paranormal. When asked if she had ever sensed a presence, the girl opened up like a faucet. She went on and on about a girl named Sarah whose spirit remained in the house after she died. What was so bizarre was that nobody had ever mentioned to this young woman that a girl named Sarah had lived and died in this house years ago.

One final note, in the Dimmick room, on a chair rests a little old fashioned doll, which seems to wreak havoc with some guests. Some people are so afraid of this doll's appearance they have actually turned her around to face the back of the chair. Diane said she can't understand why people think this doll is so evil, but she confessed that on occasion when the room has remained empty, she has found the doll's head in different positions.

Author's note: Some time after this interview, Linda had the good fortune of bumping into Dr. Tripp's wife. For the first time Linda had the chance to tell her about the sighting of her husband in the parlor. Mrs. Tripp stated that it couldn't have been her husband because he never wore flannel shirts. She went on to say that it was probably Dr. Tripp's father who was also a doctor and who was usually seen wearing flannel shirts.

The Village Green Inn
Falmouth, Massachusetts
508-548-5621
800-237-1119

FORGET ME NOT

Light and bright seems to be the theme of the Wildflower Inn in Falmouth, MA. White walls, honey colored hardwoods and oversized windows give one a sense of relaxation and comfort. A wrap-around porch and beautiful gardens also add to the Inn's ambiance.

Donna and Phil Stone purchased the Victorian house in 1995. It had sat vacant for five years and had fallen into disrepair. The Stones did massive renovations, turning what was once a private residence into what is now an award winning five-guestroom bed and breakfast. The deed on the house is dated 1910, but a postcard with a picture of the house dated 1898 was sent to Donna by the daughter of a previous owner. The exact age of the house remains unknown to this day.

Donna told me that shortly after they bought the house they began renovations. It was during and after that time that some very strange and unexplainable events took place.

During renovations one of the workmen claimed someone tapped him on the shoulder. When he turned no one was there.

Two months later another worker claimed someone tapped him on the hip. Again, no one was there. The workman then asked Donna if anyone hid his tools during the night. Apparently, the workers' tools were frequently and unexplainably moved from one place to another during the night.

At that point in the interview Donna's eighty-five year old father walked in. He takes care of the beautiful gardens and lives on the property. He claims the ghost frequently likes to rearrange his pool balls. He said, "Almost every night I purposely leave them neatly arranged in specific order. The next day I am astonished to find them scattered all over the table." Donna's father believes the ghost is very friendly and most definitely is not afraid of it.

There is one room in particular that seems to be the center of the Inn's ghostly activity. All the guestrooms are named after flowers. This room is the "Forget Me Not." Donna recalls a gentleman who stayed at the Inn for a short time while visiting his daughter. At the time he was alone, his wife was not flying in until the weekend.

The first morning he came down for breakfast and asked Donna if she had been upstairs last night. Donna replied, "No." He then asked if Donna was a runner. Again, Donna replied, "No." Next he questioned, "Did you have a guest check in late last night?" Donna said, "Why are you asking all of these questions?" The man replied, "At 4:15, I woke up and heard what sounded like a nylon running suit swishing together." He then found himself staring face to face with a girl in a lengthy dress with long light hair. He said to the girl, "Can I help you?" She then turned and left, but he never saw or heard the door open or close. It was as if she walked right through the door. This went on for three nights in a row. At exactly 4:15 every night the same girl appeared. The man was fascinated but never once felt any fear.

That weekend his wife had flown in to join him. He told Donna that he was not going to mention the experience to his wife. The next morning the couple arrived at the breakfast table, she said to Donna, "Did you happen to come upstairs last night?" Donna replied, "No." "Well," she said, "it must have been a dream. At 4:15, I thought I heard a rustling noise and I could have sworn there was someone in the room."

The very next day Donna and her husband awoke at exactly 4:15. The "Forget Me Not" is right above their bedroom. They both heard footsteps and water running. The next morning Donna asked the couple if they slept well. The gentleman replied, "We slept extremely well, we didn't even see the ghost." Donna said, "I thought I heard you walking around early in the morning." The couple replied, "Neither of us awoke during the night."

Donna noted that after each guest checks out, one of the most important rituals is to make sure the alarm clocks are turned off in each room, as to not wake the next guest. For some reason in the "Forget Me Not" room and only in that room, the alarm clock inexplicably sounds off, even when Donna is certain it was turned off.

Research has revealed the house was once a two family home, very rare for that era. At the time the "Forget Me Not" room was actually a dining room. Donna was informed that a young girl had died in the house, but that is all the information she has for now.

The Wildflower Inn
Falmouth, Massachusetts
508-548-9524
800-294-LILY
(5459)

REMEMBER ME

One warm spring evening, I traveled up to Brewster, MA for an interview with Ruth Manchester. Ruth and husband Cliff are the owners of the award-winning Bramble Inn and Restaurant. The Inn is located in two different historic buildings. The main Inn was built in 1861 and is home to their critically acclaimed restaurant, considered by many to be the finest on the Cape. In addition, there are three lovely guestrooms located on the second floor. The 1849 house, just a short stroll from the main Inn, boasts another five rooms.

When I first arrived, Ruth and I sat in one of her elegant dining rooms. We then began to discuss some of her most unusual and fascinating ghostly tales.

These stories contain material not only on the Bramble Inn, but on another Inn formerly owned by the Manchesters, known as the Pepper House. In addition, I have also included a story on a house Ruth lived in before they bought the Bramble Inn.

Now I know what you're thinking: why am I including a story about a house when the book is supposed to be about Inns? Well, trust me, it all ties in.

Ruth and husband Cliff purchased a house in the town of Brewster in 1980. It was a relatively new home, but she was informed by someone that the house was thought to rest on an ancient burial ground.

Immediately after they moved in, Ruth noticed the master bedroom always seemed a bit cooler than the rest of the house, accompanied by a strange odor. Her cats had the run of the house but the master bedroom they dared not enter. After spending four happy years in the house with their three young daughters the Manchesters began negotiating to buy the Bramble Inn. The house was then put up for sale in October of 1984 and sold the following April. Papers were passed on the Bramble Inn and the Manchesters departed their home and moved into the Inn.

It was during the time when they put their house up for sale that an unbelievable turn of events began to take place. One night Ruth remembers walking up to her bedroom and getting into bed with her husband and hearing a dog bark. Suddenly, Ruth and Cliff were surrounded by ghostly apparitions hovering above their bed. She said they appeared to be misty human figures of men and women dressed in Puritan-type clothing. This was not a one-time event. These apparitions appeared nightly until the house was sold. At times they were so shaken by these ghosts, they tried sleeping with the lights on. However, this did not seem to work as the misty figures kept reappearing night after night. Ruth said, "We never felt threatened by them, I guess it was a feeling of sadness. Maybe because we were moving to another house and they were going to miss us." I asked Ruth if she could remember exactly what some of the apparitions looked like. She replied, "My husband and I distinctly remember one of them. It was a man who had a pointed beard and wore a curved metal helmet, like Ponce de Leon."

After the Manchesters moved into the Bramble Inn, they never saw the ghosts again. But not long after, another presence was felt in a guest-room in the 1849 house. She said, "I used to get a creepy feeling sometimes when I entered the room." Apparently, she was not alone. Over the years, several of the guests have reported feeling a presence in this little room and to this day chambermaids are terrified to clean it.

Back in 1987 the Manchesters purchased another Inn in Brewster called the Pepper House. It is a beautiful Federal Style Colonial built by Captain Bangs Pepper in 1793. They owned the Pepper House until 1996 when it was sold to another couple.

Before the Manchesters purchased the Pepper House Inn, it had been an antique shop for 30 years. After heavy restoration, they converted the house into a delightful bed and breakfast. It sits almost directly across the street from the Bramble Inn on Route 6A.

For a time, the Manchesters relocated from the Bramble and took up residence in the Pepper House. One night a couple had checked in. They were staying in room number five, directly across from the room Ruth was residing in. The next morning the couple came out of their room frantic. They said they heard horrific pounding on their door, as if someone was trying to enter. The couple said they started screaming at whatever it was to go away. The pounding persisted into the night. They became so terrified they actually moved a large highboy in front of the door. When they finished telling Ruth the story they quickly checked out, saying the Inn was too haunted for them to stay any longer.

The Manchesters were shocked. They heard absolutely nothing. Not a sound all night.

Another incident that took place in room number five happened to a couple on their honeymoon. After they checked in, the couple claimed to have felt a presence in their room. The husband said, "Whatever it was, I had never felt anything like it. It just didn't seem to want me there. It was really making me nervous," he stated.

Ruth told of a story early on that I thought I would save until the very end. Right after they bought the Pepper House, as I mentioned, the house needed major restoration. One day Cliff was pulling out an old kitchen sink. Under the sink were old decrepit floorboards that needed to be replaced. As he started to pull up the old boards, he noticed something silvery and blue. It was an old ring. Now remember, in the beginning of the story I told you of how Ruth's original house was going to tie in? Well, I wasn't bluffing. When the two of them examined the ring closely, their mouths dropped. There was a figure etched into the blue stone. It was the man with the pointed beard and the curved helmet that hovered above their bed for so many months. To this day Ruth still wears the ghostly ring. Mysteriously, it was a perfect fit.

The Bramble Inn & Restaurant
Brewster, Massachusetts
508-896-7644

THE VANISHING WALL

In the previous story we discussed Ruth Manchester's experience with the Pepper House and the Bramble Inn. Believe it or not she is back for more. There is an Inn right down the street from her Inn on 6A, known as the Old Manse Inn. It's a very large beautiful house that dates back to the year 1801. The house was built by a Sea Captain known as Winslow F. Knowles.

In 1979 the Inn was purchased by Ruth's husband's parents. They operated the Inn for a number of years and just recently sold it to Ruth's daughter, Suzanne, and husband David. I was

informed Suzanne and David worked extremely hard restoring the Inn and their efforts should be applauded. The spacious common rooms are beautiful and I hear their restaurant has quite a following.

Now I'm going to take you back a few years back to when Ruth's in-laws owned the Inn. Ruth's husband's great aunt claimed that the downstairs bedroom was terribly haunted. She always sensed a presence and refused to stay in that room, now by the way a pretty cocktail lounge.

One time Ruth and husband Cliff were managing the Inn while her in-laws were on vacation. Ruth told me of a shocking story that happened to her one night, while sleeping in the supposedly haunted downstairs bedroom. She stated before she went to sleep she began to sense something, possibly a presence. The wall in the bedroom was facing her side of the bed. Behind that wall was a hallway leading to the kitchen. In the middle of the night Ruth was awakened by a strange noise. When she sat up, she found herself gazing right through the wall next to her bed. Ruth said, "It was like the wall had completely vanished and I was starring into the hallway." If that wasn't enough, a ghostly apparition of a young girl wearing a faded pink nightgown materialized. She appeared to be carrying a candle and slowly walking down the hallway toward the kitchen. Ruth leaped out of bed, but as soon as her feet hit the floor the apparition disappeared and the translucent wall suddenly became solid once again. Ruth said, "I don't think it was a dream, I know I was awake."

Old Manse Inn
Brewster, Massachusetts
508-896-3149

THE GHOST UNDER THE STAIRS

While driving home one evening, via 6A, I spotted the Beechcroft Inn (Brewster, MA) and decided to do a little investigating. I had recently heard about their restaurant and when inside I asked the waitress to see a menu. Before I left I casually said to the waitress, "By the way, do you have a ghost?" She replied, "You'll want to speak to Celeste about that."

One morning I met with Celeste at the Inn. Over a hot cup of coffee and a delicious piece of cinnamon cake, we began to chat about her Inn and resident ghost named Toby.

The Beechcroft Inn had its beginnings in 1828 as the first Universal church in Brewster. Eventually, the Congregation moved to a larger church, which is now the Brewster General store. The original structure was converted into an Inn in 1854. Over the years the Inn bore many names. When it was known as the Tip Top Inn it played host to Arthur Fiedler for many years.

Unfortunately, the Inn had fallen into disrepair during the 90s until Celeste Emily and husband Bob purchased it in 1995. They worked diligently restoring the Inn as well as its reputation. In my opinion, they did a wonderful job. The ten guestrooms are

The Ghost Under The Stairs

bright and cheerful and decorated with interesting period antiques. You will find the dining room intimate, even a bit romantic, and the cuisine is simply out of this world.

When Celeste and Bob first moved into the Inn, they immediately sensed a presence. Their dog, a cocker spaniel appropriately named Joe Cocker, would often bark frantically when Celeste was cleaning the rooms. "It was as if the dog was actually barking at an unseen presence," she stated. Over a short period of time this ghost, whom they now call Toby, began making himself known.

During their first winter they were visited by Celeste's dentist, Becky, and husband Adam. They drove up from Rhode Island and were staying for a couple of days. They were residing in room number 2. The first night, Adam went to sleep before Becky. When Becky finally retired, she walked up stairs got undressed and climbed into bed. Suddenly Adam woke up and stared at the window. He then said, "Becky, what are you doing? Why are you standing by the window? Come to bed." What Adam didn't realize was that Becky was lying beside him. She shot up and said, "I'm right here." Horrified and hearts pounding, they both found themselves starring at a ghostly apparition. At that moment Becky felt a hand on her back and it wasn't Adam's. They both screamed and jumped out of bed. The figure then vanished. They described the ghost as a tall figure wearing a long white robe and believed it to be a man.

Another couple staying in room number 2 came down for breakfast one morning and said to Bob, "Do you know you have a ghost?" Bob replied, "Yes, we do, why?" The couple then told of a man in a long white robe standing by the window in the middle of the night. And once again the woman reported feeling something touch her on the back.

Celeste remembers a party from New York that once stayed at the Inn. They were attending a wedding and as she put it, not the friendliest of people. She said she believed Toby really hated these people. Right after they checked out, the housekeepers were astonished to find the pictures in the hallway had been thrown down the stairs. When they looked into the room the party had vacated, the pictures where all over the floor, as if they had been tossed in an angry rage. One picture had completely disappeared all together. Miraculously none of the pictures were damaged in any way. Celeste believes that Toby was just showing his discontent, but didn't mean any harm.

One of the waitresses employed by the restaurant has reported hearing heavy footsteps when she has been in the storage closet beneath the stairs. Strangely, no one ever seems to be around at the time.

Celeste and Bob believe that Toby might have been an old Minister, since the house was originally a church. He is thought to reside on the second floor in a cozy storage closet under the stairs. Celeste said, "It's just a feeling we all get, we really believe he lives there."

Beechcroft Inn
Brewster, Massachusetts
508-896-9534

A Pat on the rump

I believe if Inns could speak this one would chuckle and say "find me if you can." Living on the Cape and being quite familiar with the Dennis area, even I needed explicit directions. With directions in hand, I still managed to get lost, winding up at Cape Cod Bay and wondering "Am I even close to this place?" After turning around and finding the left I was supposed to take, I finally found the Dennis Inn.

The setting is one of tranquility: a sprawling weather-shingled colonial set on spacious grounds, surrounded by manicured shrubs and blooming spring time flowers. The Inn's décor, with its decadent fireplace, detailed woodwork and pretty color scheme of soothing blues and soft whites is sure to please the fussiest of patrons.

The house dates back to 1928, originally built as a private summer home. In 1947 it became an Inn and restaurant. The Inn is now owned by Linda Garland and Sebastian Falcone. They operated the business for the first four years as an Inn and restaurant and began specializing in functions. Sebastian stated that over time they enjoyed the function part of the business so much they slowly began phasing out everything else. Today the Dennis Inn strictly caters weddings, various types of functions and private parties.

After a brief tour I said to Sebastian, "I understand your Inn has a ghost." Sebastian replied "You say ghost, we just use that word because we don't know how else to label this."

Sebastian said when he first purchased the Inn, odd little things began to happen. At first he kept it to himself until his staff began mentioning funny little things that they were experiencing as well. That's when everyone began sharing their stories. They all came to the realization they might be sharing the Inn with a ghost.

Sebastian said that a magazine once did an article about their ghost. After receiving many letters from people inquiring about the ghost, he received a startling phone call. The woman started by saying, "I just want you to know I'm not a nut. In fact my niece lives right next to you. I have a story I think you might be interested in." The woman said she used to summer at the house (the Dennis Inn) back in the 1940s. Apparently, one of her sister's husbands was a pilot during World War II. He was shot down, captured and imprisoned in Germany. One day out of the blue, the family's maid said, "your husband is out of prison." The woman made an inquiry about her husband's release at the Veterans Administration. No one had any information about his release. Two and half days later the Veterans Administration called the house. They just received word that her husband had escaped from the German prison camp. To sum it up, it was the woman's theory that the maid was clairvoyant and after reading the article in the magazine she came to the conclusion that it is probably the maid haunting the Dennis Inn.

I asked Sebastian to go into some detail about the ghost. He began by saying, that every so often when he climbs into bed at night he feels the other side of the bed go down as if someone has just joined him. Apparently, this began happening from day one and still continues to this day.

Sebastian recalled when Linda's mother was out in the yard one day cutting flowers. She took her gloves off, put her scissors on the gloves and went in for a little break. When she returned to the yard the scissors were no where to be found. About a year later Sebastian needed an end table that was stored in the attic. When he picked up the table he heard something sliding in the drawer. He put the table down and opened the drawer. Incredibly, inside were the scissors Linda's mother had lost a year ago.

Sebastian's son had a little run in with the ghost as well. Wanting to move to the Cape, his son had driven down to the Cape one evening for an interview the next morning. While he was sleeping he was awakened by a cold draft. He climbed out of bed, closed the window and went back to sleep. Once again he was awakened by a cold draft. The window he had closed was now wide open. His son was so frightened that he left in the middle of the night leaving behind a short note that said, "Dad, I'm in Hyannis. I'll meet you in the morning."

The Inn once employed a bartender who used to scoff at the notion of the Inn harboring a ghost. Sebastian said he was a handsome body builder with a big ego to boot. One evening after the bar had closed the bartender was in the wine cellar stocking up for the next day. While bending over, grabbing some bottles he felt a pat on the rump. Thinking it was a waitress, he quickly straightened up and turned around. He was astounded to find himself completely alone. He walked out of the wine cellar with eyes as big as saucers. He was now a believer. He even went so far as to name the ghost. He called her Lillian after his step-mother, whom he despised.

The Dennis Inn
Dennis, Massachusetts
508-385-6571

GANGSTERS AND GHOSTS

When Ed Maas purchased the Orleans Inn in the summer of 96, saying he had his work cut out for him would most definitely have been an understatement.

The house was originally built in 1875 by Aaron Snow II for his wife and seven children. He was the direct descendant of Constance Hopkins, who was the very first person to spot Cape Cod from the Mayflower as it sailed near Provincetown in 1620.

The home first became an Inn and restaurant back in the 1940s. Apparently over the years it had many different owners and at one point was even controlled by gangsters, the Irish

Mafia to be exact. The Inn actually has a secret office built into the wall where hoards of cash used to be hidden.

Over time the Inn fell into terrible disrepair. The building had become so dilapidated that parts of it were considered unsafe.

That's when owner Ed Maas and son Ryan came to the rescue. They purchased the Inn from the bank in 1996 and started what turned out to be a massive restoration project. After they poured two million dollars into the structure and furnishings, the Inn had its grand opening in May of 1997. Ed credits his son Ryan – now General Manager – for overseeing the project, including the interior decorating.

Every inch of this 22,000 square foot Inn has been remarkably restored. Casual elegance seems to be the theme. The guestrooms are all tastefully decorated and their restaurant is adorned with mahogany tables and a beautiful fieldstone fireplace. The restaurant and lounge have spectacular water views. It's just a wonderful place to kick back and relax.

Have I mentioned any ghosts yet? Well, follow me as we climb to the top of the Inn, up to the cupola. Be careful not to bang your head; the staircases are becoming narrower and steeper. Well, we finally made it. Take a look at that exposed wooden beam. That's where Fred the bartender hanged himself in the 1950s. Now I'll take you to a little storage closet down below, where Paul the dishwasher hanged himself. And right outside the Inn, just before you walk in, is where two prostitutes were murdered in the 1940s. It's no wonder the Orleans Inn has had a reputation for being haunted for so many years.

Hannah and Fred are thought to be the two ghosts responsible for some of the bizarre incidents that have transpired in the Inn over the years. Unsure of the prostitute's name that was murdered, the Maases named her Hannah. Fred was the bartender that hanged himself in the cupola. Hannah apparently loves to play with doors. Ed explained that during restorations the two front doors were always closed and triple bolted at night. Every morning the Maases would arrive and to their astonishment would find the two doors wide open. The doors on the second floor would also be found open, after they had been locked as well.

During the construction, one of the workers laying flooring kept hearing a cat. Ed assured him there were no cats around. The same worker also mentioned seeing a strange shadow in one of the closets and at that very moment, the door in the closet slammed shut.

About a week after the Inn had its official opening, Ed was visited by a bartender who had worked at the Inn in years past. She had mentioned to Ed that she had never seen the upper levels of the Inn at the time of her employment. At that time, the upper levels of the Inn were in complete disrepair and had been closed off. It was about midnight when Ed took the former bartender for a little tour. While walking down a hallway they both suddenly froze. The air in one particular spot became so cold the hair on both their necks stood straight up. They could sense they most certainly were not alone. They began to sense an eerie presence.

On another occasion, Ed heard heavy mysterious footsteps when he was positive the Inn was vacant. Erin, his seventeen-year-old daughter, recently heard the faint sound of people talking. She too was alone at the time.

Ed remembers hearing crazy stories from former waitresses that were employed by the Inn years ago. Occasionally, late at night in the dining room when the last guest had departed, the waitresses would blow out the candles on each table. As soon as they left the dining room to grab their purses they would return and to their amazement find the candles relit and burning brightly on every table.

Another former waitress once told Ed that something had happened to her years ago that she will not soon forget. One night after the bar had closed she was gathering her belongings and getting ready to lock up. She was alone at the time. As she was leaving, she playfully said "goodnight Fred" referring to Fred the ghost. At that very moment, out of the darkness, a voice said "gooodnnnnight."

Orleans Inn and Restaurant
Orleans, Massachusetts
508-255-2222

"IT'S NOT THE DEAD THAT WILL GET YOU. IT'S THE LIVING YOU HAVE TO WATCH OUT FOR."

It started out as one of those cloudy, damp spring days New Englanders are all too familiar with. I knew I had passed the Barley Neck Inn several times while driving to Nauset Beach in Orleans, MA, but I figured I'd play it safe and call for directions anyway.

When I arrived I was informed that Joe would be a little late, so I relaxed at Joe's Beach Road Bar and Grille, one of two restaurants at the Inn. It is a great little place to spend some time. The restaurant has a lot of character with its original wide pine floors, field stone fireplace and magnificent mahogany bar. I was told it was an old barn at one time.

When owner Joe Lewis arrived, I had a hunch it was going to be great fun exploring the Inn and listening to all the interesting stories that accompanied it. As it turned out, I was right.

The original structure was built in 1848 by Isaac and Mary Doane. It started out as a two room, two story Greek Revival. After losing her husband, Mary Doane sold the house to Captain Joseph Taylor in 1866. He added more additions to the original house over the years, greatly expanding the structure. Captain Taylor, a native Cape Codder, set a record for traveling across the Atlantic in a clipper ship from New York to Liverpool in 13 days, one hour and 25 minutes.

When Captain Taylor died in 1906, the home was sold to the Gundry family and then eventually to Arthur and Dorina Nicoli. They were the first family to turn the home into an Inn. They added motel units in 1965 and turned the original part of the Inn into a gourmet restaurant. Unfortunately by 1990 the Inn had fallen upon hard times. It was eventually sold at a bankruptcy auction to the current owners, Joe and Kathy Lewis, in 1994.

While Joe was giving me a tour of the original part of the Inn, which by the way is home to their critically acclaimed restaurant, I was informed that guests staying at the Barley Neck reside in the motel units connected to the older part of the Inn. The original guestrooms are currently being restored and will be ready for occupancy soon.

When the Lewis' first bought the property it was in desperate need of restoration. One day Joe's carpenter was tearing out a wall. During the process Joe heard the carpenter yelling for him. He ran over, looked inside the wall and there standing vertically was a fully made bed. Joe said jokingly, "I think the carpenter was looking for human bones. Fortunately, none were found."

Shortly after Joe and Kathy began their renovations they started conducting interviews for wait-staff positions. Some of the waitresses interviewed had worked for the previous owners and informed Joe that the Inn has a ghost. He was a bit skeptical and took the stories with a grain of salt. During the renovations and interviewing process, the Lewises lived in the Inn for nine months alone. During this time, Joe and Kathy began believing the waitresses might be right. Doors and windows that were closed would mysteriously be found open. Lights that were turned off would be turned back on.

Joe had converted one of the rooms upstairs into an office. One day he was sitting with the door closed when without warning, the door flew open, accompanied by a cold draft. At that moment Joe knew he was not alone. He began to smell a sweet fragrance as if a woman wearing perfume was standing beside him. Joe said, "I know someone was there, and I think it was

probably a woman." Immediately after that experience, Joe stated, he was a little shaken. He said he remembers calling his mother and telling her about the ordeal. His mother calmly replied, "It's not the dead that will get you, it's the living you have to watch out for."

I asked Joe, before I concluded the interview, if anything unusual has ever happened to the waitresses. He paused and said "I remember being warned from more than one waitress about how the ghost would flip the dinner trays out of their hands, sending them crashing to the floor." Apparently, this was not an uncommon occurrence. So, if you happen to be having dinner in the Barley Neck Inn's main dining room you will never see a dinner tray being carried by the wait-staff. Now you know why.

The Barley Neck Inn
East Orleans, Massachusetts
800-281-7505
508-255-0212

SUSAN

When asked to describe The Simmons Homestead Inn (Hyannis Port, MA), one would not be hard pressed for words. Comfortable, friendly, and exotic are a few adjectives I would certainly use. In fact, it was one of the most unique Inns I have ever visited. Instead of colonial or Victorian décor, the guestrooms are decorated in exotic animal themes. When you call to reserve your favorite room, you don't say "I'd like room #3", instead you'd say "I'd like the zebra room, or possibly the elephant room." The Inn features twelve guestrooms, some with brass and canopy beds, but all with warm and colorful décor. The Inn has evening wine tasting year round and in the winter you can sip single malt scotch by the fire. If you're a scotch buff, ask to see Bill's collection. You won't believe your eyes.

This New England farmhouse was built in 1820 by Savannah Simmons. His son who lived in the house became a famous sea captain. In fact he was the youngest sea captain to obtain a sailing license to sail all seven seas. He was nineteen years of age.

The home was owned by two other families over the years and at one time was actually a potato farm. It remained a private residence until 1988 when Bill Putman purchased the property and converted it into a bed and breakfast. Bill, a former geologist and racecar driver, proudly displays the hood of a Datsun 280Z driven by one of his competitors. Who was this competitor? Well I'm not sure if anybody has ever heard of this guy: his name is Paul Newman.

After a tour of the Inn, Bill and I sat down to discuss Susan, their adorable seven-year-old ghost. Susan was a member of the Simmons family who drowned in the pond out back in 1833 at

the age of seven. Bill recalled his first experiences with this charming little ghost. When he first moved into the home in 1988 they were doing some remodeling in one of the back hallways when suddenly an apparition of a little girl appeared. She was about 4 feet tall with light brown hair and a long white dress. Bill assumes it was the dress she was buried in. No facial expressions were visible but the sound of a child giggling was clearly heard. Bill had no idea what her name was until one day a guest staying in room number five said, "Do you know you have a ghost?" Bill replied, "Yes, I do, how did you know?" The woman said, "Well, I was up all night talking to her and she told me that her name was Susan." Other guests that have stayed in room number five have also reported experiencing a strong presence and feeling a cold blast of air from time to time. Obviously, this was Susan's old bedroom.

Apparently there is an attic that runs across the house. One part of the attic was built before Susan died and the other part was added when an addition was put on in 1842, well after Susan had died. There were a couple of crude bedrooms in the attic, which Bill had restored and rented out to a few girls over the years. All have had experiences with the ghost in the attic. One girl in particular would often go to the library and take home a children's book. She would then go up to her bedroom in the attic, sit on the bed and read aloud. Bill said, "you could actually see a depression in the corner of the bed, as if a small child had sat down."

The attic was obviously a place where Susan used to play, but she has only been seen in the old part of the attic. Remember that the new part was built after she had died. Bill said, "She probably doesn't even know it exists."

The Simmons Homestead Inn
Hyannis Port, Massachusetts
508-778-4999
800-637-1649

CAPTAIN, IS THAT YOU?

In the heart of historic Sandwich Village sits a grand old 1829 Federal style Colonial Inn known as the Captain Ezra Nye Bed and Breakfast. When strolling by, the Inn seems to emanate a certain warmth and charm. Take a peek inside and you will understand why. The Inn boasts seven tastefully decorated bedrooms. Each room is in impeccable condition, complete with period antique furnishings. The Inn has a beautiful Sea Captain's room, a cozy sitting room and elegant dining room.

Elaine and Harry Dickson bought the Inn in the mid 80s and have been charming guests ever since. They are originally from New Mexico.

Elaine Dickson, a very warm and colorful person, cordially greeted me when I arrived. After chatting for only a few minutes, I quickly came to the realization these were very special Innkeepers.

Elaine toured me throughout the entire Inn, including the attic where the name Captain Ezra Nye appears in chalk on an old plank. She then led me out to a lovely sun porch where we both sat. I listened as she began to speak about the history of their Inn.

Captain Ezra Nye was born in Sandwich, MA, in 1798. By the tender age of ten, his adventures in sailing had already begun. When he reached the age of twenty, he was commanding his own ship. Captain Nye commanded five ships, all Packets, carrying mail and passengers between the east coast and Liverpool. Each new ship was larger and more luxurious than the one before and established new records for elapsed time and crossing.

The Captain married in 1826 and constructed the house in 1829. Actually this was his second house, the former was built two years earlier directly across the street and is now part of the Daniel Webster Inn.

"Now about the ghost," exclaimed Elaine. It was about 10 years ago when a man named John came to the Inn for a rather lengthy stay. He was an engineer overseeing a large project in the area. It was in the dead of winter and there were no other guests. Elaine asked John if he would mind if they got away for a few days on a little vacation. He said that was fine and the Dicksons left for a couple of days. While they were gone a friend of John's, a businessman from California, needed a place to stay while he was in town. John replied, "I'm sure they wouldn't mind," and John and his friend spent the night alone in the Inn. John's friend slept in the room known as the gold room. This is when the trouble began. As the man crept into bed he noticed the other side of the bed begin to move as if someone sat down. John's friend was absolutely horrified, afraid to move. All of a sudden, the sound of a heavy shoe or boot was heard dropping on the floor; seconds later, the sound of another shoe crashed to the

Captain, Is That You?

floor. John's friend was terrified, obviously never experiencing anything like it before. When the Dicksons arrived back from their vacation, they were immediately informed of this unusual story. They could not believe what they were hearing.

I asked Elaine if anything else has ever happened. She said neither she nor Harry have ever had an experience with the ghost, but two guests have reported feeling "ghostly breezes" at the exact same time in different rooms; one of the rooms was in fact, the gold room.

Captain Ezra Nye House
Sandwich, Massachusetts
800-388-CAPT
508-888-6142

No Bones About It

When gazing upon the Liberty Hill Inn (Yarmouth Port, MA) for the first time, one is overwhelmed with a sense of grandeur. The tall columns in the front attached to a wrap around veranda speak of Greek Revival.

The Inn features nine traditional bedrooms, a lovely sitting room as well as an elegant dining room. Spacious rooms, high ceilings and period furnishings seem to give the Inn a rather luxurious flavor.

When I approached the door I was promptly greeted by Beth Flanagan. Beth and husband Jack are the proprietors of the Liberty Hill Inn. Beaming with pride, Beth toured me throughout the entire Inn. After the grand tour, I was seated in the dining room where we began to chat about the history of the Inn.

Beth stated, "I think it was just the right time to try something different." The Flanagans, both marketing consultants from New Jersey, bought the Inn in 1986 with absolutely no experience operating a Bed and Breakfast. They had to rely solely on marketing and public relations skills. This was no easy task in the beginning, but after a relatively short period of time they became masters of their trade. The Flanagans have acquired so much knowledge over the years, they now conduct sold out seminars teaching new innkeepers the business.

The Inn has quite an interesting history. The house was constructed in 1825 by Ezekial Hallet, who at one time owned an entire fleet of ships. It was originally built by shipwrights, as signs of joining are present in the construction. The grounds of the Liberty Hill boasts the first Liberty pole, which was erected in the 1700s to defy British rule as the Revolution approached.

The Flanagans have restored an historic barn on the grounds. Four special rooms have fireplaces, a balcony and a whirlpool. Interesting artifacts were unearthed during construction. Old hand forged nails, horseshoe and pottery shards are a few of the artifacts that have been found.

I asked Beth if the Liberty Hill Inn was haunted. She replied, "All of our doors are lined with copper sheeting; when the wind blows it makes a very eerie sound that has unnerved a guest or two." She also stated that there have been numerous ghost stories reported about the Inn over the years, but they are unconfirmed and Beth did not wish to comment on them. Although, there was one bizarre story she said she could confirm. Beth said the house was first converted into a Bed and Breakfast in 1983. During the Inn's restoration, the former owner was staying in New Jersey. One day he received a startling phone call from the Yarmouth Police Department. The officer said, "All work has to be halted immediately." The owner, obviously shocked replied, "What happened?" The contractor had informed the police that he had just removed a human leg bone from the inside of one of the third floor walls.

Liberty Hill Inn
Yarmouth Port, Massachusetts
800-821-3977

DINE WITH A GHOST

I can't remember how many times I've driven by the Old Yarmouth Inn (Yarmouth Port, MA) over the years, or why I've never stopped by. I was recently informed the Inn had just changed hands and decided to drop in one Saturday evening to sample their fare.

If it's superb, creative cuisine, a cozy atmosphere, and a courteous staff you've been searching for, this Inn is a must! When you arrive, introduce yourself to Arpad and Sheila, two of the friendliest, most attentive innkeepers you'll ever meet.

Listed in the register of historic places, the Old Yarmouth Inn is one of the oldest Inns on Cape Cod. The Inn was built in 1696 and served as a stagecoach stop for many years. An original guest book dating from 1869 is on display for the guests' enjoyment.

Guests arriving for dinner will be seated in one of the Inn's three formal dining rooms or, for a more casual evening, try the rustic tavern. You probably should have a reservation, but if you don't, not to worry, you'll have a splendid time sipping a cocktail or a fine wine by a blazing fire. Have a second glass and you'll wish they never call your name. Arpad, a noted wine connoisseur, has put together a sensational wine list and is always eager to educate the neophyte.

Owners Sheila FitzGerald and husband Arpad Voros purchased the Inn in 1996. Knowing how old the Inn was I simply had to ask if they had a ghost. They were told by the previous owners that the Inn was haunted. Arpad said they really didn't pay much attention to their warning and more or less brushed it off. That was then; rest assured Arpad and Sheila are now believers. They both began sharing some of their experiences with me one night by the fire.

Sheila stated that the first person to have a run-in with their ghost was her sister. It was early one morning when Sheila's sister, Maureen, came downstairs to make a cup of coffee. As she was about to enter the dark kitchen she began to hear noises. Frightened that someone might be in there, she threw open the door, turned on the light and found the bread mixer operating by itself.

One evening after hours Arpad, Sheila, and Maureen were all relaxing in the tavern, when suddenly they began to hear a groaning howling sound coming from the inside of the wall. At that point the walls and windows began shaking and rattling. Sheila said it was almost indescribable, they had never experienced anything like it.

The ghost also seems to play little tricks including plucking wineglasses off the rack, sending them crashing to the ground. Arpad also recalls seeing an ashtray jump off the top of the pile and slide down the entire length of the bar by itself.

I forgot to mention something, The Inn rents out four of its rooms to guests, which brings us to our final story. One morning a guest awoke and walked downstairs to get a freshly brewed cup of coffee. The coffee is always kept in the kitchen and the guests are asked to help themselves. When the guest arrived at the kitchen door, she was a little confused about which door to enter. Restaurants usually have two doors, one for exiting the kitchen and one for entering. Not being familiar with restaurant doors she wondered which door to enter or why the doors didn't have handles, when from out of nowhere a disembodied voice from beyond uttered "Push."

Old Yarmouth Inn
Yarmouth Port, Massachusetts
508-362-9962

Dine With A Ghost   **65**

THE 3RD FLOOR

In the town of Centerville rests this lovely mansion. The current owners have requested that I withhold the name of the Inn for various reasons.

Brian and Sal bought this beautiful home in 1986. It had been on the market for approximately five years before they converted it into a Bed and Breakfast.

After a handful of jellybeans, Brian and I sat down in the living room to discuss their most unusual resident.

Brian said, "The first time we had contact with the ghost was about a month after we had bought the home. A woman was sitting across from me in the living room, about where you are sitting now. She turned and stared at me for a few moments and then in a quiet voice said, "Do you have a ghost?"

"You see her too?" another woman said, sitting on a bench in the same room. Brian was stunned; he did not see anything. The two women swear they saw a woman standing on the staircase dressed in old clothes. She was standing on the staircase, turned, walked upstairs and vanished.

Things remained quiet for a while until one day another woman said to Brian, "Do you know you have a ghost on the third floor?"

Brian replied, "I wasn't aware of any ghost."

The woman said, "Well I feel a definite presence in my room, but it is very peaceful and not to worry."

The next report of the ghost came from a man staying with his two sisters. He had just lost his wife. One sister had just lost her husband and the other sister had cancer. They had decided to take a vacation together, touring New England and staying in the Inn for a few days.

The woman with cancer was staying on the third floor. She said to Brian, "Do you know you have a ghost on the third floor?"

Brian's normal response had become, "Not that I am aware of."

"Well you do," she said "and she is very kind. She sat on the bed, comforted me and told me not to worry."

Another time, a woman going through a divorce also reported

being visited by this ghost in the same comforting manner. She also was staying in a room on the third floor.

Brian said this ghost on the third floor only appears to women and often women that are in need of comforting. She is described as being kind and gentle but has not been seen as of late.

I was about to conclude the interview when Brian said, "Now I'd like to tell you about my experience with another ghost in this Inn. A ghost we managed to get rid of."

He began by saying, when he and Sal moved into the house before it actually became an Inn, loud footsteps could be heard walking up and down the stairs during the night, accompanied by doors rattling and shaking. Sal said he could feel a strange presence coming from the cellar and sensed they may have a ghost. Brian knew someone in the field of paranormal. He arranged for this person to visit and give her honest opinion of what was happening. She said, "You do have a ghost and he is living in the cellar." She also felt that the ghost was of German Jewish decent. She informed them, he wasn't a disturbing presence, but he was very troubled and afraid.

Brian asked, "What do we do?" The woman said she felt this presence was bothering Brian and since he had recently suffered a heart attack, the ghost most certainly had to go.

One night the psychic returned with some special herbs and candles. She waited for the exact right moment and then headed into the cellar. The psychic then made contact with the ghost, coaxing him out of the cellar and persuading him to leave by heading into the light. Instead of leaving, the psychic caught the ghost heading down the corridor. Finally, she was able to convince him to pass on but before she did, Brian said he actually saw the ghost peering into the doorway. He said, "It looked like a gray shadowy figure with no distinguishing traits." It was of human height, but he could not tell if it was male or female. Suddenly it just vanished and was never seen or felt again.

Brian said, "I forgot to mention something." On the evening this ceremony was performed, Brian's niece and nephew had come to witness this event. They were curious, but skeptical about what was about to take place. While they were waiting for the right time to begin, the small group was having a discussion about the paranormal. In particular, they were talking about how perceptive cats were to the paranormal, when seemingly out of nowhere a terrifying cat screech was heard in the back of Brian's chair. Brian nearly jumped out of his skin. Everyone in the room heard it. The psychic asked if there was a cat in the house. Brian replied, "Absolutely not, I have never seen a cat in this house. I don't even like them."

Brian and Sal have tried to research who these ghosts might be, but without much luck. The house dates back to 1881 and has had various owners including the Catholic Church, where nuns resided. In fact one of the guestrooms on the first floor was actually a chapel at one time.

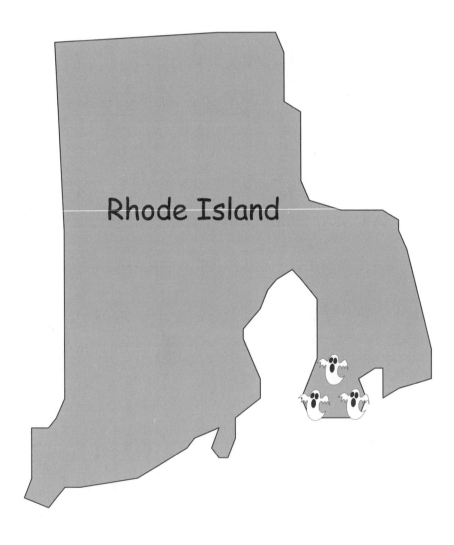

Rhode Island

MARY POPPINS

As I approached the Brinley Victorian Inn (Newport, Rhode Island) the sounds of laughter and joy emanating from the porch could be heard a mile away. "What should we do today?" "Let's tour the mansions." "I'd like to do some shopping." "Let's have another cup of tea before we go."

I must admit making my way to the front door was no easy task. Guests had rearranged the wicker furniture, almost blocking the entrance. They seemed to be having such a wonderful time conversing and nibbling on their croissants, I felt like I was intruding. "Maybe if you could move that chair a little sir...no...alright...Madam, if I could just squeeze...sorry, I'll try another way." Well, after some maneuvering I finally made my way to the front door. Upon entering, I was warmly greeted by owners John and Jennifer Sweetman. The Sweetmans purchased this turn of the Century Victorian home in 1993. The Inn is actually two houses adjoined. The one built in 1850 harbors seven guestrooms, the other, built in 1870 has ten.

As I toured the Inn, it became apparent that no two rooms are alike. The regal front parlor is adorned with Victorian

wallpaper and satin lace window treatments. The furnishings are quite formal but comfortable. There is also an authentic fainting couch for the guests' enjoyment.

Just a short stroll down the hall will take you to the Inn's relaxed library. A perfect spot to research some of Newport's fascinating history.

As wonderful as the atmosphere is here, it simply does not compare with the charming innkeepers themselves. John and Jennifer, who are both from England, go above and beyond for their guests. I merely mentioned the fact that I was thinking about visiting the English countryside, when suddenly they both became travel consultants wanting to help plan every aspect of my trip. My only regret was that I didn't have more time to share with them.

After my tour, I sat in the front parlor and listened closely as Jennifer spoke about their unusual happenings. Jennifer stated the first spring they spent at the Inn made them think the Inn might possibly be haunted.

That spring, the Sweetmans remember renting out a room to an elderly couple. At the time, there were no other guests. John and Jennifer were upstairs in their room when they heard the front door slam followed by the sound of someone running up the staircase. This was in turn followed by a rattling sound coming from the bedroom doorknob. They both just stared at one another. John walked out of his room and downstairs to investigate. He could find no one.

During the interview the Sweetman's daughter, Anna, joined us. Anna said one time a housekeeper and she were about to clean room 8. When they knocked on the door they heard the sound of paper bags being crinkled and people moving about. They unlocked the door and found themselves staring at an empty room. Anna also mentioned that in room 8 they would frequently smell wood burning for no apparent reason.

One time while in that very room, Anna began talking to the ghost. "Are you a boy or a girl?" she asked. Suddenly, coat hangers began wildly banging together. Anna said it couldn't have been the wind because every window was closed.

Another incident the Sweetmans recall involved little

chocolate mints. After the rooms are cleaned, mints in green wrappers are placed on the pillows. Frequently these mints would just disappear. And, one time when a plumber punched a hole in the wall in Anna's room, 20 unopened mints in pristine condition fell out of the wall.

Jennifer thought it was possible they had mice and hired an exterminator to investigate. The exterminator examined the house and assured Jennifer they did not have a pest problem.

After hearing the news, Jennifer walked into a bedroom and said to the ghost. "If you take any more candies, we're going to go bankrupt." Unbelievably, not one mint ever disappeared after that.

A guest staying in room 10 came down for breakfast one morning and asked, "Do you know you have a ghost?" The woman said before she went to sleep, she took her mints off of her pillow and placed them on the night table. She then heard one of the mints drop on to the floor. She reached over, picked the mint up and put it back on the table. The woman stared in amazement, as she witnessed the mint slowly slide across the table, as if someone was pushing it, and fall back to the floor.

Other guests staying in room 10 have reported hearing footsteps around their bed and feeling as if someone had just walked by.

One guest upon entering their room found their bed had been pushed into the middle of the floor. Strangely, Jennifer had just checked the room minutes before and found nothing out of place.

The morning I arrived, John and Jennifer told some guests that a writer was coming to interview them about their haunted Inn. After a brief discussion, some of their guests went to their rooms to gather their belongings. Moments later one of the guests walked downstairs and said, "My clothes are all over my room." The Sweetmans scurried upstairs. They were shocked to find every drawer wide open and clothing pulled out and dropped on the floor. Some furniture had been moved as well.

John spoke of his own personal experience, one that will remain etched in his mind forever. While alone in the Inn, John was standing on a ladder doing some touch up work to a ceiling in a guestroom on the second floor. While he was working he began to hear footsteps coming up the bottom staircase. He peeked out of the bedroom and saw a woman hunched over walking up the second staircase on the way to the third floor. John jumped off of the ladder to get a closer look but the woman mysteriously vanished. He said he could actually hear the stairs creaking under her feet as she walked. He described her as wearing a long black, Victorian dress and pointed boots, just like Mary Poppins.

There is an old black and white photograph of a woman that hangs in the library. Jennifer said it came with the house, no one ever really paid any attention to it. Sometime after John's sighting, they hired a woman to help out around the Inn. While in the library, the woman said, "I see you have an old photo of Mrs. Brown."

"Who?" Jennifer said.

"Mrs. Brown," the woman replied. "She used to own this house years ago. I cared for her in a nursing home before she died."

Jennifer took the photograph of Mrs. Brown off the wall and handed it to me. The photo depicts a woman hunched over, walking up the porch steps. She is wearing a long black, Victorian dress and black pointed boots, just like Mary Poppins.

The Brinley Victorian Inn
Newport, Rhode Island
401-849-7645
800-999-8523

FOOTSTEPS

In the heart of downtown Newport, nestled amongst historic homes and quaint shops, rests the charming Black Duck Inn.

The Inn was built in 1898. At the time it was considered a blue-collar working man's duplex. Present owner Mary Rolando purchased the Inn in 1994. She is credited for transforming this home into the elegant beauty that stands today.

Upon entering through the bright yellow door, you'll encounter the inviting front parlor where a Laura Ashley theme becomes evident. The room is enhanced by a few antique pieces, including grandfather clock and of course a hand carved black duck.

Adjacent to the front parlor is the informal dining room where a tasty continental breakfast is served on pretty blue tablecloths.

The Inn has six comfortable guestrooms, all traditionally decorated. What makes this Inn so appealing other than its charming décor and friendly staff is its location. Situated on a quiet street in downtown Newport, the Inn is only a short stroll from Newport's fine restaurants and quaint shops. Newport harbor is another exciting attraction where glorious yachts from around the world can be viewed and photographed.

If you're wondering what the name Black Duck means and even if you're not, I am going to tell you anyway.

The Black Duck was actually an infamous rumrunner vessel that smuggled liquor into Newport Harbor in 1929. It gained much notoriety with local townspeople, but was despised by the US Coastguard. When the Coast Guard finally caught up with the Black Duck they opened fire killing some of its crewmembers. Upon hearing the news local citizens were so enraged they took to the streets attacking members of the Coast Guard. Cries from the public rang out, as they demanded swift action to be taken against the Coast Guard. Even the President of the United States took notice.

When I first spoke to Linda Farrell, Mary's assistant, I inquired if the Inn had a ghost. Linda said they feel they do. First off, she wanted to make clear their ghost is a little mischievous but very friendly.

Linda said one activity their ghost seems to enjoy is throwing the deadbolts into the locked position on various doors throughout the Inn. She stated many a time she has been alone in the Inn only to find doors deadbolted when she clearly remembers leaving them unlocked.

The ghost seems to like to tinker with lights and alarm clocks as well. One time when the Inn was empty every alarm clock in all the guestrooms sounded off at once.

Lights have been known to suddenly turn on immediately after they have been turned off. One guest claimed that every time his wife left their room the light in the hallway would begin to flicker. He said with an uneasy tone, "It didn't happen to me, only to my wife."

By far the most common occurrence is the sound of heavy footsteps. "Like someone walking with boots," said Linda. They are frequently heard when guests are asleep or when the Inn is vacant. Neither Linda nor Mary seemed to be frightened by this presence. They just feel it's a former inhabitant reminding them that they are not alone.

Black Duck Inn
Newport, Rhode Island
401-841-5548
800-206-5212

HOUSE OF SPIRITS

The Inn at Shadow Lawn (Middletown, Rhode Island) lies just beyond the hustle and bustle of downtown Newport. The driveway entrance is quite impressive, giving one the sense of privacy and elegance.

I must confess I was not prepared for the world I was about to enter. I have traveled extensively throughout New England, touring Inns of all shapes and sizes. I would emphatically say that I have never been more awestruck or more inspired by an Inn.

The home was built in 1856 by architect Richard Upjohn for Hamilton Hoppin and his bride. It claims to be the first Italianate stick style home built in the United States.

The décor is sinfully rich, reminiscent of a grand European mansion. The walls wear vibrant colors and are adorn with impressive artwork from across the globe. Ancient sculptures from Italy rest comfortably atop historic Victorian furniture. The library with its dark mahogany woodwork and wall covering made of elephant skin, yes, elephant skin, give the room a grand flavor. There are even decanters filled with port and sherry, perfect for a little nightcap. Magnificent stained glass windows are found in both the dining room and the library. Rumor has it, they just might be Tiffany.

In the mood for a little dancing? The newly restored ballroom will play host to various functions including weddings and private parties.

The grand staircase meanders up three floors where the Inn's twelve guestrooms are located.

Present owners Selma Fabricant and son Randy purchased the Inn back in 1994. They have been diligently restoring it back to the marvel it once was.

Randy informed me that the Inn has an extensive history. As I mentioned earlier, the home was originally owned by Hamilton Hoppin. The Hoppins were a prominent family, well known throughout New England. Hamilton's brother was a writer and illustrator for famous authors such as Harriet Beacher Stowe and Mark Twain. Other members of the family included doctors, lawyers, senators and governors. Detailed information about family members as well as old photographs have been uncovered, that is with the exception of one person, Hamilton Hoppin. Randy said he couldn't understand why it has taken him so long to unearth information about this person. Apparently Hamilton was a very wealthy man who retired at the age of 32. He was a lawyer and businessman. It was said that during the Civil War he held government bonds and manufactured ammunition. Whether he sold to the North or the South has never been revealed, but the house was part of the Underground Railroad. Two underground tunnels exist; the entrance remains hidden somewhere in the house.

The Hoppins owned the home until the 1890s, when it was sold to the Perry family. The Perrys were responsible for having the library walls covered with elephant skin.

They say you're no one in Newport unless your house has ghosts. Let me assure you, this house has its share.

Before the house was purchased, Selma had a dream the house was haunted. That dream turned out to be true. Three psychics have gone through the house. Each of them revealed a number of different entities from the attic to the basement.

Randy said that during restoration, he would be overcome with the sensation that someone was watching him, particularly in the dining room.

The grand ballroom was Selma's old bedroom before it was restored. One morning Selma had a visitor. Upon opening her eyes, she found herself staring at a Narragansett Indian. He was standing at the foot of her bed, dressed in full war paint, and held a tomahawk in one hand. Selma quickly closed her eyes. When she opened them the Indian put his tomahawk down and vanished into thin air. Research has revealed that an old Indian path ran directly through the center of the house and down to an estuary.

One time while the Fabricants were away on vacation an older housekeeper remained to look after the house. The woman reported seeing two gentlemen dressed in Victorian attire walking with a black child. They walked out of the ballroom, looked around and then directly at her. The threesome walked back into the ballroom and mysteriously disappeared.

Randy informed me of a séance that was held at the Inn one evening. In front of the psychic performing the ceremony was a glass of water. Randy said he remembers, during the ceremony, looking around the room and then back at the glass. Suddenly, the glass began spinning around in a circle completely by itself. During the ceremony, no one felt as if they could get out of their chair. It was as if some force was holding them down. Finally at one point, Randy managed to break free. He walked into the hallway to get some air when he said he felt like he hit a wall. Whatever it was, it was so powerful it actually knocked him out of the hallway and into the dining room.

Guests have also experienced strange happenings. Doors opening and closing by themselves have been reported. Some have even felt a hand touch them on the shoulder. One time a gentleman said to Randy, "Can I ask you, is your Inn haunted?" The man explained how his little daughter kept having a conversation with, as she put it, the funnyman.

Another interesting story involved a perfume bottle. A guest reported seeing a small bottle of perfume slide across the dresser.

After that incident, Randy had a psychic go through the entire house. When she finally reached the guestroom where the perfume bottle slid across the dresser she stopped and said, "I smell lavender. There was an argument in here and a perfume bottle was thrown against the wall." Keep in mind Randy said nothing to the psychic about any of the strange occurrences guests have reported including the incident with the perfume bottle.

A former owner of the house informed the Fabricants that she once saw an apparition of a woman floating in one of the bedrooms.

I said to Randy, "You have quite a few spirits living with you." He said, "One time we gave one of our chairs to a friend and a ghost actually went with it. The recipient of the chair said they now have a ghost."

The only slightly dark or ominous part of the house is the basement, where Randy resides. Supposedly there are six different entities in one part of the cellar alone. During the Civil War, slaves were hidden in the cellar and tunnels; many took ill and died. Randy said, "We really don't know whether slaves were helped, or hidden and sold. I really don't know, I only hope they were helped."

The Inn at Shadow Lawn
Middletown, Rhode Island
401-847-0902
800-352-3750

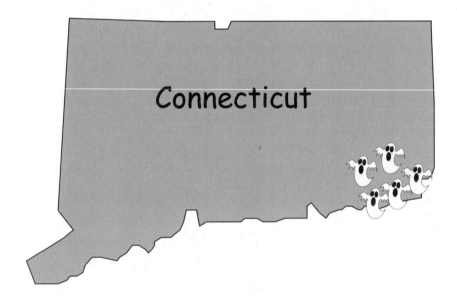

Connecticut

MURDER IN THE
GREAT WEST ROOM

It was the 18th Century; two Revolutionary war soldiers who were best friends were carousing in a tavern. The room was known as the Great West room. A quarrel broke out between them over a woman. Soon, the quarrel erupted into a hellacious fight. One of the soldiers plunged a knife into the other one. Blood streamed from his quivering body, covering the tavern's wooden floor planks. The soldier lay dead, slain by his best friend.

An attempt was made to remove the bloodstains from the floor. In those days, sand was commonly used to clean hard wood floors. The effort failed and supposedly the floorboards were flipped over and nailed back down, in order to conceal the gruesome sight.

At the time, a man named John York owned the tavern. The structure, built in 1741, was originally York's private residence. It was transformed into a tavern when the Revolutionary War broke out. George Washington was rumored to have slept here. Eventually the tavern was turned back into a private residence and over the years changed hands a number of times.

In 1996 the home was purchased by two young scientists, Leea and David Grote. After months of restoration the home was transformed into a four guestroom Bed and Breakfast and is now called the John York House.

Visiting this historic home and spending time with the Grotes is just plain old-fashioned fun. If asked to describe the Inn, I would use the adjectives charming, authentic, warm and inviting. The Inn has a comfortable atmosphere; you certainly don't feel the need to remove your shoes when you enter. The home has managed to maintain its 18th Century flavor thanks to the Grotes. The living room is quite informal with soft comfortable furniture. Old pewter, books and antiques are found throughout the room. The keeping room, just off the kitchen, is where breakfast is served. This room has a massive hearth and authentic beehive oven which is used to bake breads and pies. The four guestrooms are furnished with antique dressers and tables, reminiscent of an earlier time.

Innkeepers David and Leea are a pleasure to spend time with. Down to earth and very sweet, they make the John York House what it is.

The Inn is set on a small working farm surrounded by acres of woods and nature trails. You'll see roosters, goats and a cow named Cindy meandering about.

When the Grotes first applied for a Bed and Breakfast license, the zoning board commissioner asked how they were going to handle the ghost situation. Hauntings at the John York House have been documented as far back as the turn of the Century. The ghost is thought to be a Revolutionary War soldier, possibly the one who murdered his friend.

There may be another ghost. Historical papers reveal that a drunken guest fell down a back staircase and broke his neck. Various articles have been written about former owners and their experiences with these spirits.

During the 1950s, the owners of the house reported hearing strange noises, feeling cold sensations and seeing shadows in the back staircase. When the house was sold in 1963, the new owners decided to have a séance after having their own unusual experiences. This turned out to be a terrible mistake. Something happened after the séance, something that wasn't good. Suddenly, furniture began tipping over. Footsteps were heard walking through locked doors and a barometer in the living room had a habit of unbolting itself from the wall and shooting across the room, landing unbroken on the floor.

The most frightening occurrence involved one of the owner's sons. One night he awoke in a state of panic. When his parents walked into his room they were horrified to see red hand marks around his throat as if someone was trying to choke him.

The owners decided something had to be done. They called in a professional ghost buster who performed an exorcism. This revealed the spirit to be a man in a revolutionary war uniform who was exhibiting temper tantrum behavior. After the exorcism things began to quiet down. The last incident the couple reported was hearing three loud bangs, almost like cannon fire.

The Grotes have had a few strange occurrences as well. Before they opened the Inn for business, a friend came over for a visit. Suddenly, the glass window in her minivan exploded, scattering shards of glass all over the driveway. David said it couldn't have been heat-related because it wasn't a particularly warm day and several windows were left open.

Leea also said she distinctly remembers someone at 4:00 am repeatedly calling her name from the bottom of the staircase. When the Grotes investigated, they found no one.

One day a woman from New York had arrived for a short stay. At the time the Inn was vacant, so Leea toured the woman around, allowing her to pick the guestroom of her choice. The woman walked into one room, stopped and said, "This is the room I want, this was the children's room. I can hear them playing in here." The hair on the back of Leea's neck stood up. In that guestroom, if you look carefully, you will see tiny handprints of children in the original plaster. Upon entering, the woman never looked at the walls. The handprints were pointed out to her only after she made that statement. Someone informed Leea the woman from New York was in fact a psychic.

The John York House
North Stonington, Connecticut
860-599-3075

The Ghost of John Randall

As the autumn leaves began to peak, thoughts of the Connecticut countryside danced in my head. This was my first visit to North Stonington and I could not have chosen a more harmonious day. Sweet smells of autumn filled the air. Vibrant colored leaves set against a backdrop of deep blue sky was a sight to behold. Jack-o-lanterns and scarecrows were visible in every doorway and window. Halloween was in the air. A perfect time to visit Randall's Ordinary.

I arrived about 10:00 in the morning, a few minutes before the manager. It was time to do a little exploring. First on my list: visit the Inn's farm animals. Cricket, an adorable donkey. is always at hand to greet new arrivals. Just behind Cricket's pen is a musk ox named Rusty. At first glance his horns are intimidating, but I was assured this handsome beast is quite docile.

Randall's Ordinary is set on 27 acres of lush farmland. One could spend an entire afternoon strolling woodland trails or searching for bits and pieces of history. Bullets from historic battles have been plucked from trees, and old family graveyards await your discovery.

The working farm that dates back to 1685 is still in existence today. Most employees, no matter what position they hold, are expected to pitch in and help around the farm.

You're in for a treat; we're about to enter the dining room. Sit back and close your eyes for a moment. Allow your senses to come alive. Can you smell the smoky scent of wood burning in the open-hearth oven? Can you taste the smoky flavor of ale soaked ham or roast duckling dripping with sweet juices? Let your hands grasp the warm crusty honey oatmeal bread just removed from the beehive oven. Tear into it; allow yourself to be intoxicated by the heavenly aroma. To dine at Randall's is to experience Colonial cuisine at its finest. Set in a romantic 17th Century atmosphere, your fare will be served by wait staff dressed in colonial attire. You will view employees stoking the fire of the open-hearth oven where breakfast, lunch and dinner are prepared. If the ground is covered by a blanket of snow, listen for

the sound of horses trotting. What could be more joyous than an after dinner sleigh ride through the placid countryside?

In order to explore the fascinating history of Randall's Ordinary, we must creep back to the 17th century. On May 28, 1629, a man named John Randall was born in Bath, England. His father, Matthew Randall, was the Lord Mayor of Bath.

John married a woman named Elizabeth Morton. Shortly after, he moved to London where he became a prosperous silk merchant. When the Dutch threatened to invade England, John, his wife and child followed Elizabeth's brother, Sir William Morton (founder of New London, CT) to the New World in 1667. He first settled in Newport and then Westerly, Rhode Island.

John purchased a parcel of land in Stonington in 1680. John Randall the second built the existing dwelling on the same parcel of land. Over the years the farm was enlarged at different times according to the deed recorded at Stonington. John Randall the 3rd was a captain in the Continental Army during the war of Independence. Lt. Colonel William Randall commanded at the battle of Stonington during the war of 1812. His regiment, the 30th Connecticut, prevented British troops from landing on the Boroughs of Stonington in 1814. It is believed that this particular battle may have been the turning point of the War of 1812.

Following two terms as Governor, Alexander Randall was appointed Ambassador to Rome by his friend, Abraham Lincoln and was later Post Office General of the United States during Andrew Johnson's Presidency. Later generations of Randalls were among the first to free their slaves and became abolitionists. There is a trap door in the hearth room, which leads to a secret room where slaves were hidden.

The Randalls sold the farm in the late 1800s. In 1926 it was purchased and meticulously restored by Harvey Perry. In 1987 it opened for the first time as an Inn. It is now owned by the Mashantucket Pequot tribal nation.

The Mashantucket Pequot Tribe has done a remarkable job preserving the Inn and its surroundings. The original farmhouse John Randall built looks exactly the way it did back in the late 1600s. The 270-year-old floors squeak and groan as if they have their own tales to tell. The Inn has a total of 15 guestrooms.

Three are located on the second floor over the dining room. The other 12 are in a barn built in 1819, which was moved from New York State by a previous owner. The guestrooms are traditionally decorated, many with canopy beds, hand made blankets and period furniture.

No 17th Century Inn, no matter how beautiful, is complete without a ghost. The spirit of John Randall is alive and well. Guests have reported seeing a tall, slender, gray haired man dressed in a uniform. He wears a sad expression and holds a blunderbuss (early firearm) in his hand. One guest witnessed a small child clinging to his leg. The spirit is said to reside in room 12, above the dining room, the Randall's original home.

A psychic was once hired to investigate room 12. She said she could feel the spirit hiding in the closet. A housekeeper, while in room 12, said aloud, "You've shown yourself to everyone else, show yourself to me." The housekeeper noticed the light on the wall began to flicker off and on. "That's not good enough," she said. Suddenly, the entire light fell off the wall and crashed to the ground. She refused to enter room 12 ever again.

Staff members have reported turning lights off at night only to find them turned back on. Even one of the managers has experienced something he can't quite explain. One dark night he was driving past one of the family graveyards on the property. Suddenly, he thought he saw a person pass in front of his car. He began looking around but could find no one.

In the fall of 1997, management received a letter from a couple who had previously stayed at the Inn. At first he thought it was a complaint letter, until he read on.

In November of 1995, the couple checked into room 11. When it was time to go to bed the woman for some reason became hysterical, wanting to flee the room. Her husband actually had to read to her in an attempt to calm her down. The couple said if they had their own vehicle they would have left that night.

Two years later the same couple returned to the Inn with friends. This time they stayed in room 12, the other two couples resided in rooms 10 and 11.

After dinner at the Inn all three couples met in room 11. While they were talking the water in the bathroom sink suddenly turned on by itself.

At the end of the evening the couple returned to room 12 and got ready for bed. As her husband was dozing off, she heard a noise by the attic door. It sounded as if someone was tumbling down the steps and hit the door. At the very same time the latch on the door began to move up and down. She had a strange sensation that someone was watching her through a gap atop the attic door. Her friend in the next room heard similar sounds at exactly the same time.

Exactly which John Randall may be haunting the Inn, is not clear. The answer may lie in the blunderbuss the ghost was seen holding. As previously mentioned a blunderbuss is a very primitive firearm dating back to the 16th and 17th centuries. John Randall the first would have been the person most likely to have used such a weapon.

Randall's Ordinary
Landmark Inn & Restaurant
North Stonington, CT
860-599-4540
860-599-3308

A Woman in the Attic

Set in the picturesque town of North Stonington, Connecticut lies a charming Victorian Inn known as Antiques and Accommodations. The property is owned and managed by Tom and Ann Gray.

The 1860 house harbors 3 lovely rooms while the 1820 house next-door features two spacious suites; one has two bedrooms, and the other has three.

The Inn's décor is quite decadent, adorned with early English and American Antiques. Hepplewhite, Chippendale and Queen Ann pieces are found throughout the Inn. Guests will enjoy a bountiful candlelit breakfast served on fine china in the elegant dining room. Specialties include chilled cantaloupe soup, a two-cheese egg soufflé with fresh vegetables, or a stilton and aquavit omelet with dill remoulade.

The Inn is surrounded by lush gardens and narrow walking paths. Close by are numerous streams and ponds perfect for a picnic lunch. If you're still craving more, take a leisurely walk around the quaint country town of North Stonington. You won't hear cars tooting their horns or see traffic jams here. Instead you're apt to hear the sound of children giggling or view people walking their dogs or vice versa. There are no outlet stores or expensive boutiques and restaurants are few and far between. The residents will tell you they wouldn't have it any other way.

I was informed that two elderly people died in the 1860 house, six months apart. Their son died in an accident shortly after.

Ann purchased the two houses in 1980. When she took over the property she began restoring the 1860 house which is now the main part of the Inn. During renovations mirrors and paintings would mysteriously, as Tom puts it, shoot off the wall and crash to the ground. Fortunately for the Grays, this no longer happens.

Another occurrence that still happens to this day involves a guestroom that was once the front parlor. On occasion at about 2:00 or 3:00 in the morning the room will be inundated by the smell of cigarette smoke. No one has been able to detect where it comes from.

Guests have also reported hearing strange noises, but Tom isn't certain if the sounds are those of an old house or something else.

The most startling event to date occurred in the attic of the 1820 house. There are four old unfinished rooms that used to be occupied at one time. One evening Tom was doing some work in the attic. He left the room and remembers leaving a light on before he went to church. At about 9:30 in the evening he was walking back from church, when he looked up and saw a woman in a long Victorian dress walk in front of the window. At the time there was only one guest staying on the first floor of the 1820 house and she said it wasn't her walking around in the attic.

Tom made reference to a wall that is directly beside the window in the attic. The direction the woman came from meant that she would have actually had to walk through the wall to get to the window.

After the incident Tom asked a parapsychologist to investigate the Attic. After about an hour he reported to Tom that he felt the presence of a woman. He also mentioned the presence of two small children.

Antiques and Accommodations
North Stonington, Connecticut
800-554-7829
860-535-1736

COFFIN CORNERS

The House of 1833 (Mystic, Connecticut) was constructed by a prominent man named Elias Brown in the year, as you might have guessed, 1833. He married a wealthy woman named Elizabeth Burrows, whose family owned many granite quarries in Rhode Island. Together they raised 12 children. Elias was an attorney and the first selectman of Mystic. He also chartered the first bank of Mystic in 1833. The bank's original structure now stands at the Mystic Seaport Museum and is known as the Counting House.

This stately Greek Revival mansion was a guesthouse known as "The White House" in the late 1800's – early 1900's. In 1946, after an extensive renovation, it opened as an exclusive dress shop whose sign read: "House of 1833 Town and Country Clothes; Roy E. Smith, Proprietor." It became quite well known and operated successfully until the mid to late 1970's when it was sold and returned to a private residence. It remained a private residence until it was purchased by Carol and Matt Nolan. Carol, a financial analyst by trade, along with teacher husband Matt, decided one day to quit their jobs and become innkeepers. They went on a nationwide search for the perfect spot and ended up in Mystic. After six months of renovations the Inn opened for business in the spring of 1994.

This historic Inn is a blend of opulence and artistic nuances. The front parlor has retained the Greek Revival flavor. Formal furniture is found throughout the room, surrounded by blue walls and gold accent pieces. The room also boasts a lovely Belgian marble fireplace.

The front parlor flows gracefully into the elegant Victorian music room. Here you'll find a pristine baby grand piano, a pump organ and a 19th century crystal chandelier.

Take your time as you climb the winding, unsupported staircase up to the second floor. The curved wall along the staircase wears a colorful hand painted mural of Mystic in the 19th Century. Other interesting murals painted by the same artist are found throughout the house.

The Inn's five guestrooms are all lavishly decorated. A particular favorite is the cupola room, located on the third floor.

All this splendor is surrounded by lush manicured grounds accompanied by a Har Tru tennis court and an oversized in-ground swimming pool.

During my tour Carol looked at the staircase and said, "Do you know what those cut outs in the wall along the staircase are called?"

"Coffin Corners," I replied. Coffin Corners are cut outs in the staircase walls commonly found in 19th century homes. During that time period, people often died at home. Bodies were usually prepared and put into a coffin in the very room in which they died. If the body was on the second floor it was often difficult to maneuver the coffin down the curved staircases without destroying the walls; hence, coffin corners.

The Nolans have done extensive research on the history of their Inn, but have only uncovered bits and pieces of the Brown family history. Unfortunately Elias Brown died two years before photography was invented; however, a single photograph of a woman in her coffin was uncovered. Carol believes that the photo was of Elizabeth and that she likely died and was mourned in the house.

Just before the Inn opened for business, Carol's friend Vivian from Manhattan was helping with some finishing touches. Vivian and Carol were walking through the music room and about to enter the dining room, when Vivian gasped and stopped dead in her tracks. "What's the matter?" Carol asked.

"Oh it's nothing," Vivian replied. About an hour later, Vivian said, "you know, as we were walking through the music room and about to enter the dining room, I saw a woman standing in that doorway." Carol said she described the woman as very old with long white hair, similar in appearance to the woman (Elizabeth?) in the photograph.

About two months after opening the Inn, Carol remembers hearing a knock on the door and a woman with her elderly mother asked if they could tour the house. As it turned out, the woman's mother lived in this house when she was a young girl. As they were touring, the older woman paused in the same doorway in which Carol's friend Vivian had seen the ghost. She turned to Carol and said, "Has anyone ever told you there is a ghost in this house?" She then continued, "When my two sisters and I were young, we played in the music room and often saw an old woman standing in the doorway watching us play." Carol said the description this woman gave of the ghost was identical to what her friend Vivian had seen in the very same doorway.

About three months after the Nolans' son Alex was born, Carol remembers waking up for a 2 A.M. feeding. Though almost half-asleep on the living room couch, she began to feel a presence. Carol looked around but saw nothing. A few months later, on a very, cold wintry afternoon, Carol was in the house alone when she began to feel the very same presence. She looked up and saw a sheer white piece of fabric float by the glass etching on the door to their apartment. As soon as the fabric disappeared, so did the feeling of the presence. She believed it was "their ghost" just making sure that she and her young son were safe and warm.

The House of 1833
Mystic, Connecticut
860-536-6325
800-FOR-1833

HAPPY BIRTHDAY

Perched on a knoll surrounded by seven woodland acres sits the historic Red Brook Inn (Mystic, Connecticut). Guests will have their choice either to reside in the Haley Tavern built in 1740 or the Crary Homestead, a center chimney colonial built in 1770. Both properties have remained virtually unchanged since the 18th Century thanks to owner, Ruth Keyes.

Over a piping hot cup of hibiscus tea, Ruth and I sat and chatted by the crackling fire in the keeping room of the Haley Tavern. The keeping room was where 17th and 18th Century families spent most of the winter. It was a room that contained a large hearth where most of the cooking was done.

In 1980 Ruth purchased the Crary Homestead, converting it from a private residence into a functional Bed and Breakfast. Sometime after, she purchased the Haley Tavern, which was also a private residence, and transported the entire house to a parcel of land just up from the Crary Homestead.

The two homes are full of historic charm. The Haley Tavern features seven guestrooms, some with canopy beds and working fireplaces. Downstairs there is a gentleman's parlor where sherry

can be enjoyed by a warm fire. Not to be forgotten is the elegant ladies parlor where women can saucer and blow their tea. I will explain: let's pretend for a moment we are back in the 18th century and we're having a tea party. On the table everyone would have a teacup and saucer as well as a small plate known as a cup plate. After you pour your tea into the cup, you would then pour the tea into the saucer and rest your teacup on the cup plate. You would then blow on the tea in an attempt to cool it, and drink it directly from the saucer. That is where the term "saucer and blowed" came from.

After your tea, acquaint yourself with the old fashioned game room just off the gentleman's parlor or you may enjoy a gander at Ruth's collection of 18th and 19th century oil lamps in the ladies parlor. There's even rare Sandwich glass mixed in, so look carefully.

Guests staying will be treated to a hearty breakfast including tasty waffles and fluffy pancakes. If it's a taste of early colonial life you seek, the Red Brook Inn should be high on your list.

One would think Haley's Tavern would be oozing with spirits and ghostly apparitions, but it's the Crary House just below that is truly haunted.

Mysterious events have taken place in the North room located on the second floor. On more than one occasion guests have mentioned to Ruth at breakfast that they have felt a presence in the North room.

One couple while staying in the North room made the mistake of opening the window while a fire was lit in their room. In the middle of the night the room became inundated with smoke. The woman slept soundly, but her husband awoke only to find himself staring at a woman's face less than six inches away from his. He said it literally shocked the wits out of him. He described the woman as being elderly and having short gray hair.

About a year later another guest reported waking to a smoky room and seeing a woman with white hair wearing a dark shawl and standing in the corner with her hands folded.

So, who is this woman that haunts the Crary Homestead? Ruth believes it has to do with the death of the former owner's first wife. After she died her husband married her best friend who was much younger than she was. Ruth's theory is that his first wife was angry that he married her best friend and didn't want

her living in her house. It is the first wife's spirit that is thought to haunt the Inn.

Ruth's theory does not go unsupported. One day she received a call from the former owner's second wife. She thought it would be fun to rent out the Crary Homestead and hold her husband's 75th Birthday party there because he loved the house so much. Ruth agreed and said she could have the party in the front parlor. The woman met Ruth at the Inn to begin planning the event. Upon entering the Crary Homestead they were both overcome with a horrible odor of rotting meat. After they left Ruth had her handyman go into the basement to see if perhaps a mouse or something had died. He searched the entire basement and said there was no smell of any kind.

About three days before the party Ruth met with the woman at the Inn. Once again, upon entering, they began to smell rotting meat. "I hope it's not going to smell like this at the party," the woman stated.

Shortly after, Ruth told a friend about the horrible smell. He mentioned to her that ghosts sometimes emit foul odors. He also went on to say that the first wife probably doesn't want the second wife in her house.

The next night Ruth remembers watching Unsolved Mysteries and the subject matter was ghosts, and how they can emit foul odors. Ruth became worried, surely the ghost must be trying to sabotage the party, she thought.

The night of the party Ruth's friend was standing by the doorway of the back room having a cigarette. He said the moment the woman arrived he began to smell an odor. He said, "It was the worst fart I ever smelled." Fortunately, the odor didn't last very long and the woman didn't seem to notice.

During the party the cake was brought out and the candles were lit. It was a carrot cake, her husband's favorite, made by a famous Mystic pastry baker. As the woman began to cut the first piece she noticeably began to struggle, finally giving up. This delicious looking carrot cake was reduced to a pile of crumbs. Ruth said the inside had literally disintegrated. The entire cake had to be thrown out leaving guests bewildered while they held their empty plates.

During my visit, Ruth handed me a letter she had just received from a guest.

Sunday, Nov.15, 1998

During breakfast, our gracious hostess, Ruth, overheard the conversation my fiancée and I were sharing with other guests at the table. Ruth later asked if I wouldn't mind writing a little note about my experience.

I awoke out of a sound sleep around 1:30 AM this morning, and was unable to fall back asleep for a few hours. Upon waking, I gazed into the fading embers of the fire we lit earlier that evening and began feeling a "presence."

I went into the bathroom unafraid and continued to feel a "presence." I washed my face and just stood in the bathroom with the light on, curious about my feeling.

A clear thought came to mind: I feel the "presence" of a very powerful woman here; one who was "modern" before her time. I felt an unusual kinship with this "presence" and thought perhaps it was the woman in the painting up at the main house. I enjoyed the feeling that she "shared" with me and was not fearful at all if it became stronger. However, that was all I experienced. I lay awake in bed for a couple more hours, with my fiancée asleep by my side. I finally fell asleep and again awoke a few hours later. Considering my lack of sleep, I felt serene and pleasant at breakfast. I continued to feel her gentle "presence" throughout the morning and plan to lodge at the Red Brook Inn again!

Red Brook Inn
Old Mystic, Connecticut
860-572-0349

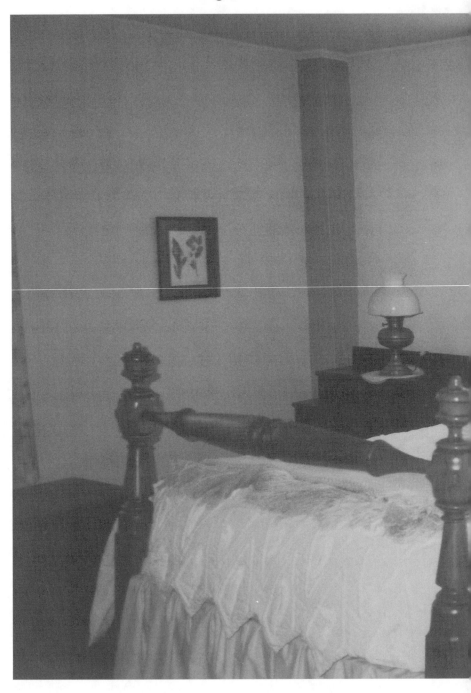

New Hampshire

THINGS THAT GO BUMP IN THE NIGHT

We'll begin our tour of the Three Chimneys Inn (Durham, New Hampshire) in the rustic ffrost Sawyer Tavern. I sat at an old wooden checkerboard table next to granite walls dating back to the 17th Century and gazed upon a menu of endless delights. Finally, I succumbed to the pressure of having to order and selected the rich and flavorful dill clam chowder accompanied by a spicy blackened chicken and blue cheese sandwich with assorted melon slices on the side. If you're more adventurous, why not sample the Rabbit potpie. Whatever entrée you choose, be assured you will not walk away hungry.

Perched on Valentines Hill, the Three Chimneys Inn lies in the quaint town of Durham, just a short jaunt from the University of New Hampshire.

In 1991 Ron and Jane Peterson rescued this stately post and beam house from a group of college students who were residing there. After a year and a half of restorations and a never-ending seven-year struggle with the Historic District Commission the Inn opened for business in January of 1997.

Upon entering through the dark green front doors you'll find yourself in the formal but cozy front parlor. In the winter you can rest your weary bones in the soft leather chairs or play a game of chess by a warm fire. Just around the corner you'll come to Coppers and Maples, the two formal dining rooms. Here you'll feast on such delicacies as pan-seared Rack of Lamb with a mint and rosemary demi-glace and Grilled Atlantic Salmon served with sweet pepper couscous, red and yellow vine ripened tomatoes and poulet glace. The dining rooms have a total of four fireplaces surrounded by Georgian décor. Don't be surprised if you see Ron or Jane scurrying around stoking the fires, setting tables or carrying dishes into the kitchen. Its refreshing to see owners who are not afraid to roll up their sleeves and get their hands dirty.

The Inn has a total of 25 guestrooms. Eight are located in the original part of the house dating back to 1649 and seventeen more in the restored 1795 barn next door. All rooms are lavishly decorated with gargantuan four-poster and canopy beds fit for a king.

A stroll around the grounds will bring you to a little pond out front. Actually it's an old swimming pool; the first ever built in New Hampshire. If you look straight across the river you'll see pristine white colonial homes where one of George Washington's generals once lived.

The house was originally built by a man named Nathaniel Hill. Hill had a King's grant of 500 acres and constructed a sawmill by the waterway. Logs were taken from the New Hampshire forest and brought to the sawmill and then shipped in gundelas to Portsmouth for export all over the world.

These spacious grounds have played witness to a tragic Indian Massacre. On July 18, 1694 a force of approximately 250 Indians under French command attacked settlements in this area, killing or capturing approximately 100 settlers. It was the most devastating French and Indian raid in New Hampshire during King William's War.

Only four families have owned the home since 1649, the Hills, Woodmans, ffrosts and Sawyers.

During my tour of the original part of the Inn, Ron said, "I really want you to see this room." In a quiet voice he said, "this room known as the Rafters and the room next to it called the Loft are two of our most active guestrooms." He went on to say when these rooms are vacant strange noises are often heard day and night. Ron said it sounds like someone walking around.

A few weeks before my visit, one of Ron's managers had an unusual experience one night. It was about 2:00 am, all employees had left and the doors were locked. The 1649 house had no guests that evening. The only person who remained was the manager, catching up on some work. While he was in his office he began to hear heavy footsteps coming from the floor above, which is where the front parlor is located. He came running up, unbolted the doors to the parlor and found himself staring into an empty room. He then walked back into his office and suddenly began to hear the footsteps once again. Nervously he dashed out of his office and into the front parlor, once again he found the room empty. This happened a total of four times that evening, leaving the manager a little shaken.

As I was about to depart, Ron informed me about a caretaker who looked after the property years ago. He lives in a house just on the edge of the property and we decided to drop in for a brief visit.

Tom Moriarty was the caretaker for approximately 20 years when the Sawyer family owned the house. He is an 85-year-old poet, sharp as a tack and has a grip that would bring a mountain gorilla to its knees.

During his tenure, Tom had witnessed some unusual happenings. He clearly remembers, when the house was empty, hearing the sound of footsteps following him around the house on more than one occasion. He has seen rocking chairs rock back and forth by themselves and recalls seeing a figure of a person while alone in the cellar.

There is an ancient graveyard that backs up to the Inn but Tom believes the ghost is someone who once lived in the house, someone who just won't go.

Three Chimneys Inn
Durham, New Hampshire
603-868-7800
888-399-9777

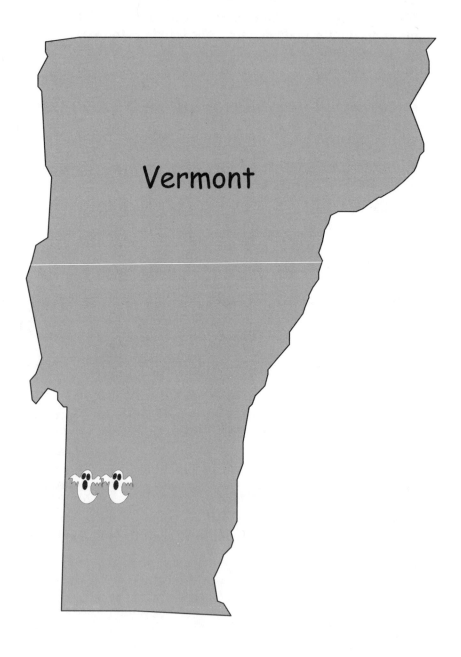

MR. DARRELL

Tucked away in a little corner of Southern Vermont, just beyond the glitzy shops of Manchester, lies the story book town of Dorset. It's a town where you can scratch a yellow lab's tummy in the middle of the road or have a quiet lunch on a wooden bench surrounded by picturesque 18th Century homes.

Not far from the town center you'll find a cluster of white clapboard buildings known as the Barrows House. In 1784 the expansive grounds were owned by the Dorset church. The Federal style main house was constructed for the Reverend William Jackson, the second pastor. In 1900 the property was purchased by Theresa Barrows and established as an Inn. Over the years the Inn has changed hands a number of times and is now owned and operated by Jim and Linda McGinnis.

Set on 12 restful acres the Barrows House is really like staying in an historic resort. Each quaint building includes a sitting room, comfortable bedding and plenty of old family antiques. There's even an in-ground swimming pool and two tennis courts to make your stay more enjoyable.

The main Inn is a mix of traditional, Queen Anne and Victorian furnishings. Other highlights include an 18th century brick hearth located in the living room and original hand painted stenciling now being painstakingly restored. Not to be forgotten, the Inn harbors a superb restaurant and tavern, set in an informal and relaxed atmosphere.

Owners Jim and Linda are history enthusiasts and community activists. They speak with great pride about the historic town of Dorset and enjoy its peace and solitude.

After I finished poking around, I said to Linda, "I'd like to hear a little about your ghost." Linda said the ghost seems to become very active at times and then becomes dormant. She mentioned there has never been an actual sighting but unexplainable events do happen. For example, I was told about the Inn's chef who was incredibly anal about how his shelves were kept. All canned goods had a precise place with labels facing forward. One time while alone, he remembered leaving the storage room and returning shortly after, only to find the shelves completely rearranged and in total disarray. Linda believes the ghost has a sense of humor and it was trying to tell the chef not to take life so seriously.

Jim told me about a time he was working at his computer late at night with his dog, named Marley. The main Inn was empty, everything had been shut down and locked up. The two swinging kitchen doors are normally left open for ventilation purposes. While he was working Jim suddenly began to hear a noise coming from the kitchen. It was the sound swinging doors would make if they were opening and closing at a frantic pace. He immediately stopped working and dashed into the kitchen. Astounded, Jim found the two doors wide open as they should be and nothing was out of place. He went back to his computer and once again the sound of swinging doors rang out. Jim ran back into the kitchen and turned the lights on, but everything appeared normal. He feels he was just being played with.

Every year the McGinnises put up a member of the Vermont horse festival for a two-week period in exchange for free advertising. They hosted the same woman for three years, when to their surprise she chose not to return to the Inn. Instead another woman from the festival checked in. On the last evening she said to Jim, "I'm going to ask you a question and I know it may sound silly, but I want you to look me in the eye when you answer it. Is this place haunted?"

Jim smiled and replied, "If you had asked me this sometime earlier in the year, I would have said no, but now I'm not so sure." Jim shared some of his experiences with her and then asked her what she had experienced. She explained that the woman who had been coming here chose not to return because she determined the Inn was haunted and too many things had happened. Jim asked her again, what she personally had experienced. The woman said she was a sound sleeper, but was awakened two or three times during her stay by someone walking up and down the hall. Jim mentioned that it was probably just him turning off the lights at night. The woman said sometimes the lights were not turned out when she heard the footsteps and mentioned that she could tell if it was Jim walking because she could see his shadow under the bedroom door as he walked by. She then said whenever this other thing walked by her door there was no shadow of any kind.

Jim took me up to the room the woman had resided in and closed the door. He then turned on the light in the hall and walked by the room. Sure enough, I witnessed his shadow in the gap under the door as he walked by.

Other incidents have been documented as well, such as a bottle of Joy that literally shot across the kitchen by itself and a waitress who swears she has seen unexplainable shadows out of the corners of her eyes.

Just recently, while Jim was catching up on his work he began to hear the sound of chairs moving across the floor in the dining room. At the time the dining room was empty, but Jim was so busy he just ignored the sound until it stopped. This incident seemed absolutely impossible because the dining room floor has wall to wall carpeting and the carpet would have certainly muted the sound. Could it have been possible that the dining room originally had wooden floors and the sounds Jim heard were from another time? There is a small picture of the dining room taken in the 1960s that hangs in the foyer. If you look carefully, you will see wooden tables and chairs resting on beautiful hard wood floors.

The McGinnises wish they had an answer as to who this spirit might be and you're probably a bit confused about why this story is entitled Mr. Darrell. You'll have to patient until we visit our next Inn, just down the road; see you inside.

Barrows House
Dorset, Vermont
802-867-4455
800-639-1620

A DISMEMBERED SPIRIT

Shaded by towering maples on the corner of Village Green, lies Vermont's oldest continually operating Inn, known as the Dorset Inn. Built in 1796 this historic Inn has been featured in such publications as *Gourmet Magazine, Town and Country, Yankee Magazine,* the *New York Times* and CNN's coverage of Christmas Getaways.

From the outside the Dorset Inn is truly stunning with its stately pillars and glistening white clapboard. Surrounded by manicured grounds and quaint stone walkways, this historic Inn is the icing on Dorset's cake.

Major additions were added in 1900 and 1947 in order to accommodate Vermont's increasing tourist population. The Inn has three floors and a total of 32 immaculate guestrooms.

When you enter through the heavy wooden front door, the room to the right is a small sitting room where the guest registration is located. Turn left and you'll enter the informal gathering rooms. This might be the only Inn where Labrador Retrievers are part of the décor. You'll view these gentle, huggable, bumbling creatures sauntering about vying for your affection. They come in an array of colors, chocolate, yellow and black and not to be forgotten is the Inn's adorable Bassett hound. Along with the labs these two rooms are furnished with antiques, knick-knacks and plush teddy bears. The country furniture is soft and cheerful and rests on pretty wide pine floors.

Sissy Hicks, owner and chef, presides over the Inn's critically acclaimed restaurant, serving approximately 200 different selections a year. Beside the restaurant, you'll find the relaxed tavern where you'll be served an array of full-bodied ales and fine liquors.

At about 4:00 in the afternoon, I asked Sissy to go into some detail about the Inn's ghost. She told me to follow her into the kitchen and start by interviewing one of the other chefs. I walked over and introduced my self amidst a frenzy of boiling pots and simmering sauces. "Sissy mentioned you had an experience with this ghost," I said in a loud voice to overcome the kitchen noise. The chef paused and stepped away from the stove. I could tell by the expression on his face that he had witnessed some unusual things. For instance, he has felt icy cold spots in the morning

when he has walked through the doorway from the kitchen into the tavern or vice versa. This is sometimes accompanied by the sensation of being surrounded by cobwebs.

He told me his first sighting of the ghost happened two and half years ago at 5:45 in the morning. He said he began to prep for breakfast when out of the corner of his eye he thought he saw a person. When he turned and looked, standing in the doorway leading out to the tavern was a gray shadowy figure with no feet or head. All that was visible was a long gray over coat and civil war jacket with two sets of buttons. The apparition was there for only a moment and then vanished into thin air. He has also played witnessed to an unexplainable gray haze that passed by at eye level while working one night in the kitchen.

Another employee caught a glimpse of a man's head with dark puffy hair and no body attached, peering in through the window in the kitchen door.

The Inn's two bartenders have also experienced some bizarre occurrences. One reported feeling an icy cold spot behind the bar that sent chills down her spine. The other bartender heard mysterious voices coming from an empty room behind the tavern. She said it almost sounded as if there was a cocktail party going on.

Some guests have reported hearing noises coming from room #32 when the room has been vacant. In particular the sounds of people walking around and furniture being moved about. The door has been found locked when it was purposely left open as well.

As I was about to conclude, Sissy inquired if any other Inns in Vermont were being included in the book. I said, I had just interviewed the Barrows House. She smiled and said in a quiet voice, "Mr. Darrell." Before Sissy bought the Dorset Inn 15 years ago, she was the head chef at the Barrows House for the previous owners.

She explained that at the same time every year an eccentric older man would come to the Barrows House for a lengthy stay. He drove a Bentley he named Barbara Bentley and a Lincoln he named Linda Lincoln. When it was time for breakfast or dinner he would always come down the back staircase and walk through the kitchen doors into the dining room and sit at the same table. One day they received the word that Mr. Darrell had passed away. Sissy distinctly remembers something strange happening the following year that would have coincided with his annual visit. While she was working in the kitchen a ghostly breeze was felt coming down and passing through the kitchen. Suddenly, the kitchen doors began to swing back and forth. There was never any doubt in Sissy's mind, Mr. Darrell had returned.

Dorset Inn
Dorset, Vermont
802-867-5500

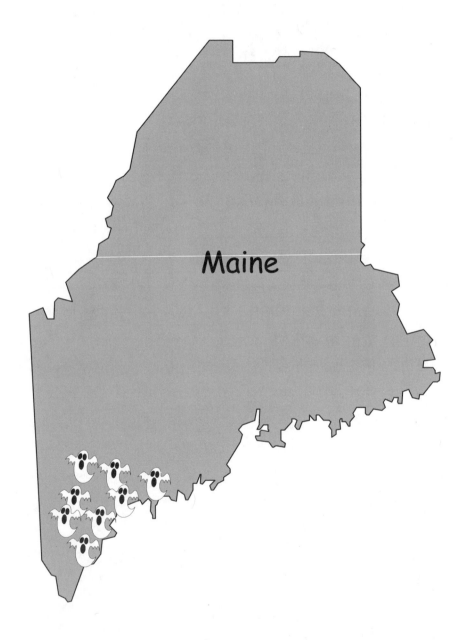

Maine

HAUNTED WITH LOVE

I must confess visiting the Puffin Inn and meeting owner Lee Williams for the first time took me back to my childhood. It was as if I was eight years old and my parents had just dropped me off at my grandmother's house. Lee reminded me very much of my grandmother, a warm and charming person with an extra large heart. She is a woman in love with her Inn and her profession.

Touring this Inn would be a joy for anyone, unless of course you dislike puffins. These little creatures are tucked into every nook and cranny. People from around the country send hand carved puffins, stuffed toy puffins and pictures of puffins. As you might have guessed, the puffin is Lee's favorite bird.

This lovely sea captain's home features eight delightful guestrooms. All are bright and cheerful with distinct personal touches. The formal living room, with its period antiques and stately furniture, is a wonderful gathering place. Guests can also take advantage of the Inn's wrap around porch, a perfect place for conversation or an afternoon siesta. The heart of Ogunquit is just minutes away, but the Inn manages to maintain a quiet and peaceful atmosphere.

In the 1980s this home was transformed from a private residence into a functional Bed and Breakfast. Lee, a retired banker, operates the Inn with the help of her husband, Maurice, and other members of the family.

It's time we leave the Williamses at least for a little while. Don't despair, we will catch up with them at the end of the story.

The first time I spoke with Lee she said it was imperative that I speak to a woman named Amanda Stevens. I was told Amanda's family owned the house and this is where she spent part of her childhood.

Before we go any further, I would like to say that some of these stories might be a bit shocking. However, you needn't be afraid, there are no malevolent forces at work here. There is an abundance of energy, but it's positive energy.

In the late 1800s the original part of the house sat on a parcel of land on route 1 in Ogunquit. It was constructed by a sea

captain named Walter Perkins. Eventually Mr. Perkins decided to relocate the house up on a hill where it now rests. At the time moving a house was quite a feat. It was loaded onto a trolley and pulled by a single horse. The climb was so arduous the horse had to walk in circles, slowly making its way up the hill.

In time additions were added, including the wrap around porch. When Amanda's family bought the house in 1969, they soon discovered the house was alive. Amanda has always thought the house loved her family, even tried to protect them at times. Often when someone would come to the house complaining about something or with an unpleasant disposition, shutters would inexplicably fall off the house in an attempt to scare them off.

The house had a back secret staircase that led from an upstairs bedroom to the downstairs, seemingly a perfect place for mischievous teenagers to sneak out at night. Not so, says Amanda. Whenever she or one of her other siblings attempted to sneak out something very frightening would happen. If the doors leading to the staircase were open, they would suddenly close. Then the light in the staircase would go out, leaving the person in complete darkness. This in turn would be followed by a cold draft. Needless to say, no one ever snuck out at night.

Amanda remembers another incident that happened in the family room. Her sister's twin toddlers were playing in front of a large oak hutch that was unsecured to the wall. As the children played, the hutch began to fall. Amanda and her family played witness to the twins being picked up by an unseen force and gently tossed out of harm's way. She said, "That's when we knew something was trying to protect us."

Amanda said that the only part of the house she disliked was the basement. She described it as a dark and clammy place where you always felt as if someone was behind you. Often when the children would open the laundry chute and look down into the basement a human face would appear. No one could tell if it was a man or a woman, it was just a face.

The attic, Amanda's old room, seemed to be another place of heightened activity. Doors would open and close and objects were often moved about. By far, one of the strangest occurrences included a picture that was hung on one of the walls. The picture depicts a young girl with long hair sitting sideways in a chair. Amanda said something used to happen to the girl in the picture, something she will never forget. About half a dozen times, and usually when she had company over, her guests would often glance at the picture, look away and then to their amazement or horror, notice the girl in the picture had changed positions and was now facing the opposite direction.

I asked Amanda if she or any family member had seen an apparition. She hesitated for a moment and said, "Yes, in the attic." On occasion she had witnessed what she describes as a human form, similar to a negative of a photograph. Whether the apparition was a man or a woman was not clear. Amanda stated that viewing this apparition was a frightening experience probably because it took her by surprise and because it had a habit of sneaking up on her from behind.

Apparently this house was also quite musical. Trumpets were frequently heard throughout the house, especially by Amanda's mother. She would scurry around the house, often with assistance of a neighbor, trying to locate where the sound was coming from. Their piano could also be heard playing a few notes by itself as well.

From time to time the entire family would hear footsteps walking up and down the staircase. Amanda especially remembers the sound of the wooden steps creaking as something slowly climbed the staircase.

The day finally came when Amanda's family sold the house. Sadness filled the air as they packed up the last of their belongings. Before they drove away Amanda's mother decided to say one last good-bye to the house. As she walked back inside, she was suddenly overcome by a horrible odor emanating from the plaster beside the staircase. Her mother feels it was the house's way of saying, "Don't go."

Amanda feels the spirits occupying the house, while a little frightening at times, always tried to show their love.

Since the Williams Family bought the house, things have eased a bit, but not entirely. Footsteps are still heard throughout the inn and phantom knocks on the back door are common as well.

In room #8, pictures are commonly removed from the wall and found neatly stacked in a little closet next to the door. Guests have also reported feeling a strong presence in this room.

Lee informed me that on occasion she will spend the night in some of her guestrooms. One time while she was residing in room #9, she felt as if the entire room began to move. Lee said, "It's hard to explain, the room felt like it was moving, but I wasn't."

Rooms 8 and 9 are the two guestrooms with the most activity. It's not surprising, after all these rooms used to be Amanda's bedroom in the attic.

The Puffin Inn may indeed be haunted, but Amanda and the entire Williams Family truly believe it is only haunted with love.

The Puffin Inn
Ogunquit, Maine
207-646-5496

A Victorian Haunting

Who among us would not be inspired by this Victorian masterpiece, known as the Nellie Littlefield House? Surrounded by manicured gardens, the home is simply an architectural delight, adorned with gracious rooms, detailed woodwork and private decks. Tastefully decorated, the Inn is a blend of soft hues and rich vibrant colors. Guestrooms are all unique, some with antiques and period furniture while others boast a more contemporary flair. The round room is a fabulous display of workmanship and should not be missed. You'll be hard pressed to find any chips or scratches in the furniture and it's no wonder since the Inn has adopted a strict no-children policy. After dining at one of Ogunquit's fine restaurants, you will be invited to work out at the Inn's on-premises fitness center. What more could you ask for?

The house had its beginnings in 1889 when J. H. Littlefield constructed it for his wife, Nellie.

J. H. Littlefield was considered a pioneer in the cottage business. He developed more than a dozen cottages and studios strictly for rental income.

The home was occupied by the Littlefield family for a number of years. The last member to depart was a gentleman named Roby Littlefield, born in 1888. In his day Roby was a prosperous man and played an important role in Ogunquit's history. He served in both the State Senate and local government. He was a noted conservationist and received much notoriety for getting the legislative approval of the Ogunquit Beach district. This meant the village could acquire the beach and dunes for public access. So, the next time you're sunbathing or taking a romantic moonlight stroll on scenic Ogunquit beach you know whom to thank.

Roby actually lived to be one hundred years of age, remaining in the house well into his nineties. He was considered eccentric and could often be seen in the window rocking in his chair as he looked out. Unfortunately, the house fell into terrible disrepair. Eventually Roby's family decided to relocate him to a nursing home where he spent his last years before he died in 1988.

When present owners Forrest and Ethel Haselton purchased the house in 1994, they completely gutted and painstakingly restored the home. It opened as a Bed & Breakfast in 1995 and is managed by Innkeepers Patty and Jorg Ross.

While we sat on the Inn's porch Jorg mentioned that just before Roby left his house he said to his nephew, "Don't change a thing, I'll be back." With that in mind, strange occurrences have transpired here. For example, Jorg said that in the middle of the night his VCR, that is only a year old, started ejecting wildly. Shortly after this occurred he took the VCR to a repair shop where it was examined and thoroughly cleaned. Once again in the middle of the night it started ejecting wildly.

I was informed the Inn has a chair lift located on the staircase for disabled people. On occasion it starts shaking and vibrating and sounds like it's ready to climb the stairs – without a soul around.

Another incident occurred in the room known as the Nellie room. The room had remained vacant for a period of time when one morning a large water spot was detected on the rug near the bed. Jorg said they were dumbfounded. They knew the room had been vacant and there was absolutely nothing that could have leaked. The carpet was literally soaking wet, completely unexplainable.

Patty and Jorg once heard one of their chambermaids report feeling as if some type of presence had just whisked by her while she was in the very same room.

On morning a woman while checking out, quietly said to Patty, "Do you have a ghost?"

Patty said, "Why do you ask?"

The woman replied, "My husband was about to enter the bathroom when he said, 'Did you just leave the room?' 'How could I,' she replied, 'I'm still here.'" Her husband said he thought he saw a woman quickly walk past him and leave the room. Stranger still, the door to the room was closed and never appeared to open even when the woman left. Once again, this mysterious sighting took place in the Nellie room.

The Nellie Littlefield House
Ogunquit, Maine
207-646-1692

ROOM 2

Nestled in the heart of Ogunquit Village rests this landmark known as the Old Village Inn. Built in the mid 1800's, this lovely New England Inn blossoms with romance and historic charm. The Inn's Victorian décor is highlighted by intricately carved woodwork and fanciful furniture. The walls are a unique blend of tasteful wall coverings and striking artwork. Interesting period antiques and other treasures are scattered throughout the Inn's seven guestrooms.

The Inn features five individually decorated dining rooms. The décor varies from sunny and light to bold and luxurious. The cuisine is excellent with a traditional New England emphasis.

After dinner, mosey into the lounge for a nightcap. Here you'll be treated to the libation of your choice, while you rub elbows with natives and tourists from around the world. It's a great way to end an evening.

The Inn was founded by a man named Barak Maxwell born in 1816. Barak built vessels for foreign commerce, the most famous being the Brig and Betsey Ames. He was also a selectman, town treasurer, superintendent of schools and both representative and state senator for Maine.

I thought it would be fitting if another writer described Barak Maxwell in his own words. "Mr. Barak, so he was always called, was a rather short stocky man, a bit bow legged. He dressed different from most Gunkiters; often wearing a Chesterfield style derby hat and a Prince Albert coat. In many ways he was Ogunquit's leading citizen." — by Roby Littlefield, editor of the Ogunquit Breeze.

Tom Shupe purchased the Old Village Inn in 1993. I had a chance to chat with him one afternoon about the infamous room #2 and other ghostly happenings.

Tom stated that room #2 certainly seems to be the center of the Inn's paranormal activity, but unusual events have transpired elsewhere. For instance, one time in the basement an employee informed Tom that he witnessed a Christmas tree stand float upward and begin to move by itself.

Tom mentioned something else that seems to be a frequent occurrence. Late at night when he has shut down the dining rooms and turned off all of the lights he notices one lamp, in the room known as the Ogunquit dining room, will suddenly turn itself back on.

Are you ready to climb the steep staircase and enter room #2? As previously mentioned, this room is the center of the Inn's ghostly activity – why, no one is certain. In fact, no one seems to know who these ghosts are.

Tom remembers hearing stories about previous owners closing the Inn down, turning off lights and driving away, only to look up and find the lights and television back on in room #2.

Stories of chambermaids having strange encounters with these spirits have also surfaced over the years. From time to time a number of guests have reported feeling a strong presence in room #2, while others have experienced a different phenomenon. Some guests have felt strange air masses rushing by them as they entered or walked near room #2.

Tom usually informs guest about their ghost if something odd is reported, but he assures them their ghost is always friendly.

The Old Village Inn
Ogunquit, Maine
207-646-7088

SEVEN DAYS AND SEVEN NIGHTS

Maggie and Wayne Carver are the proprietors of the Waldo Emerson Inn, located next to the famed Wedding Cake house in Kennebunk, Maine.

The original part of the house (now the kitchen) was constructed in 1753 by Waldo Emerson. The main portion of the Inn was constructed in 1784 by the shipbuilder Theodore Lyman, Waldo's son-in-law. It is the oldest house in Kennebunk. The structure is considered Colonial Dutch Gambrel. There are 17 rooms, 4 of which are guestrooms and 8 fireplaces. You'll find the Inn to be quite cozy and very relaxing. The guestrooms are decorated with interesting antiques and the living room seems perfect for unwinding, perhaps with a good book and a spot of tea by the fire. In the spacious dining room former inhabitants have painstakingly etched their names and dates into the original windows, so as not to be forgotten.

After a brief tour, Wayne escorted me into a little hall off of the kitchen. He then uttered, "Whatever it is, this is where it is said to reside." He was referring to their ghost and pointing to a little closet under the stairs. Every winter after the Inn closes, something rather strange begins to happen. In the evening, when the Carvers are in their bedroom, the latch on the closet door in the hallway beneath the stairs can be heard opening. Then without warning, eerie, heavy footsteps can be heard slowly climbing the creaky stairs. The footsteps always stop just before they reach the landing at the top. Then after about ten minutes the footsteps begin their descent.

Wayne questioned the previous owners about this strange occurrence and was informed they too experienced the same eerie footsteps for years.

Apparently, the house has a reputation over the years for being quite haunted. During the 1920s the former inhabitants were so disturbed by this presence that an exorcism was put forth. Seven priests came for seven days and seven nights trying to rid the house of this entity. Back then ghostly activity was rampant. The house had become a truly frightening place to live. Fortunately, for the inhabitants, the exorcism was somewhat successful in quieting things down a bit.

As I was about to conclude, Wayne said, "The only other thing we've experienced happened last week."

Wayne was rummaging through his attached mud room trying to find a flashlight that his plumber had forgotten. The room was simply too dark for him to find anything and he said to himself, "Wayne, maybe if you turn on the light you'll find it." At that very moment he heard the click of a switch. Wayne was no longer in the dark.

The Waldo Emerson Inn
Kennebunk, Maine
207-985-4250

THE CAPTAIN'S SPELL

I honestly believe I had my first out of body experience while visiting the Captain Fairfield Inn. (Kennebunkport, Maine.) No, it had nothing to do with anything of the supernatural nature. I am referring to the strawberry crepes and sour cream I sampled for breakfast one morning. They were simply out of this world.

Owner and Chef Dennis Tellagnon and his wife Bonnie are the proprietors of the Captain Fairfield Inn.

Bonnie, a charming energetic person, plays host while Chef Dennis tantalizes the guests each morning with mouthwatering breakfast cuisine.

I was only visiting briefly, but one thing became evident: these two really pour their hearts into their trade. Attention to detail is key here and it shows. Perfection is a word I would not hesitate to use.

The Inn itself dates back to 1813, a grand old Federal style mansion nestled amongst other gracious sea captains' homes. Captain Fairfield and his wife Lois were the original inhabitants of the home.

Captain Fairfield was born in Arundel, Maine in 1784. By the tender age of 22 he was sailing ships owned by Tobias Lord. Shortly after he was married at 23, he began transporting cargo down the eastern seaboard across the Atlantic and on to Europe. During the War of 1812 the English blockade of the US coast devastated the New England shipping industry. Captain Fairfield was forced to find a new occupation; he became a privateer. Unfortunately, he was almost immediately captured by the British Navy and locked away on Christmas Eve in the dreaded Dartmour Prison in England. Eventually he was released and returned to Maine to be reunited with his beloved wife in 1815. In 1820 Captain Fairfield took ill and died at the age of 36.

There is a fascinating story that tells how Captain Fairfield had his portrait painted at some unknown port in the Southern US. The portrait was intended to be a gift for his wife and sent home on the next ship departing for Maine. The painting depicts a prosperous young man holding a white envelope in his right hand. For some reason the envelope had his employer's name and address painted on it, Tobias Lord and Co., Kennebunk, Maine. Unfortunately, during the long voyage home the ship sank taking the portrait to the bottom of the sea.

Two years after Captain Fairfield's death, his former employer Tobias Lord was informed by the Captain of a Swedish ship that his crewmen had spotted a tubular tin case floating in the ocean. They retrieved the tube, opened it and inside found a portrait of a young man holding an envelope addressed to Tobias Lord and Co., Kennebunk, Maine. Unbelievably, it was the portrait Captain Fairfield had painted for his wife so many years ago. The portrait was put on a ship and sent home to his wife. Sadly, by the time it had arrived she had passed away.

The unusual oil painting managed to survive over the years and can be viewed at Brickstore Museum on Main Street in Kennebunk.

— *Portrait of Captain James Fairfield, artist unknown, ca. 1808. From the collection of The Brick Store Museum, Kennebunk, Maine.*

The Tellagnons believe the house was owned by six or seven other families before they purchased it in 1992. At the time of purchase, the Inn had fallen into bankruptcy and was closed. They worked diligently day and night restoring the Inn to the former beauty it once was.

The interior décor is considered Williamsburg Colonial / Country English. The nine spacious rooms are all uniquely decorated, giving one a sense of warmth and relaxation. The front parlor is magnificent. Rich colors, period antiques and interesting accent pieces add to the Inn's charm and elegance.

During my tour of the Inn, Bonnie began explaining how she truly feels that the Inn is possessed by the spirit of Captain Fairfield. She said, "It's just a wonderful feeling we all get. A sense of peace and harmony, if you will." Apparently, she is not alone. On many occasions guests have expressed how peaceful and relaxed they feel once inside the Inn. Many of them have said how they can't explain it, but they just feel so good during their stay.

That's not to say the Inn has never had unusual happenings take place. Bonnie mentioned that people have often reported feeling a presence, particularly in the room thought to have been Captain Fairfield's. Some even have said they have felt as if a spirit was hovering over them while in bed. One gentleman staying in another room reported feeling a cat walking on his stomach while he was trying to sleep, but saw absolutely nothing. Bonnie has felt this presence herself a couple of times. Strangely, it has occurred when she has been standing at the top of the cellar stairs.

Let's now venture down the cellar stairs as Bonnie's husband Dennis tells of his own fascinating experience.

One day Dennis needed something in the chest freezer they keep downstairs in the cellar. He dashed down the stairs, walked over to the freezer and suddenly was overcome with the sensation that he was not alone. Dennis turned to see if anyone was there and found himself staring at the ghostly apparition of Captain Fairfield. The apparition was dressed in Colonial attire and upon closer inspection the image suddenly vanished. Dennis said, "I've seen the painting of the Captain. I really believe in my heart, it was him."

Bonnie has done some research on Captain Fairfield and has in fact read some of his old letters written to his wife while he was at sea. She said after reading them, she felt strongly that the Captain was a warm and kind man.

I confessed to Bonnie that after the interview, I too was overcome with a feeling of warmth and serenity. Bonnie said, "I think you are falling under the Spell of Captain Fairfield." I think she was right.

Farewell to Home

Farewell sweet Fraserbury bay
Our gallant bark is under way
And o'er the ocean's crest we speed
Past Rattray Rocks and Peterheed
Ah, who can tell if o'er the main
I'll return to our land again
For India's shores are distant and far,
And many dangers between me are.
Should in a watery tomb I sleep
Far in the bosom of the deep
Or should I lie on foreign shore
In memory I will ask no more
But one beloved crystal tear
From my sweet Buchan maiden dear,
May providence watch o're you and
I'll think of thee when far away
James Dunn
(1836-1875)

James Dunn was Bonnie Tallagnon's great grandfather. He died at sea in 1875.

The Captain Fairfield Inn
Kennebunkport, Maine
207-967-4454
800-322-1928

THE IN-BETWEEN WORLD

I'm going to take you back in time. Back to the 70's before Bonnie and Dennis Tallagnon purchased the Captain Fairfield Inn.

After spending many years in the restaurant business, the Tallagnons decided enough was enough. Bonnie and Dennis were looking for a life style change. They had often read about people operating country Inns and became quite intrigued with the idea. The search for the perfect spot took them to scenic Vermont. After an extensive search, they found an old farm that had been operated as a rough and tumble ski lodge. They purchased the property and named it the Red Clover Inn after the Vermont State flower. They worked diligently converting the old lodge into a beautiful ten room Inn serving breakfast and dinner.

The majestic New England Farm dates back to the mid 1800's. It was eventually purchased in the 1940's by General Woodward and his wife. The 200-acre property known as the Woodward farm became a retreat for the entire Woodward family. The Tallagnons met with some of the grandchildren of General Woodward. They reminisced of wonderful childhood memories spent at the farm years ago.

During the 10 year time span when the Tallagnons owned and operated the Inn, guests would often ask if the Inn was haunted. This was due to strange and unexplainable noises heard throughout the Inn. On occasion a guest would even report feeling a presence.

Bonnie remembers one particular couple that had a unique experience while staying in Mrs. Woodward's old room. One morning during breakfast they informed Bonnie they were visited by an apparition of a woman. They described the apparition as a small, dark woman who had her hair pulled back. The spirit walked through the bedroom door, across the floor and out the window. Bonnie was astounded. She knew these people had never seen a picture of Mrs. Woodward, yet their description was identical to her appearance. This couple claimed they had a special gift. They said there is an in-between state of sleep and consciousness which enables them to tap into the spirit world.

In 1986, the Tallagnons sold the Red Clover Inn. Well, you know the rest of the story.

SOMEONE HAS RETURNED

Envision a sprawling English country manor perched on a hill surrounded by lush gardens and private courtyards. No, you haven't entered Wales or Stratford upon Avon, you've just arrived at the Harbor Watch Inn, Kennebunkport, Maine.

When you arrive via Route 9, you'll be facing the back part of the Inn where the parking lot and two restaurants are located. Stroll around to the front and you will have entered an entirely different world. You will feel like an aristocrat as you saunter through the Inn's magnificent courtyard and flower filled gardens. The private brick terrace seems to be a lovely spot to unwind. The spacious grounds, just beyond the courtyard, are perfect for family frolicking or maybe a leisurely game of crochet is in order.

The Inn's décor is one of impeccable taste. Deep greens and crisp whites prevail in the main lobby accompanied by formal yet comfortable furniture. The main dining room is enclosed in an atrium-like setting with original brick floors and majestic views of the Kennebunkport River.

For lighter fare try Martin's Brick Oven Tavern, a casual setting serving the best brick oven pizza in Kennebunkport.

The grand staircase leads to the nine guestrooms. All are sunny and bright with antiques and Victorian pieces. Honey colored hardwoods married with hand-woven oriental rugs are a nice touch. Original wrought-iron window panes give way to sweeping views of the harbor.

Now that you've had a brief tour, let's delve into the Inn's fascinating history. The parcel of land this manor now rests on was originally owned by a man named Gideon Walker back in 1745. A farmhouse was constructed on the property along with a private family cemetery.

In the late 1800s Edward Clark, grandson of Nathaniel Lord, purchased the property, building a handsome summer cottage. Unfortunately, the house caught fire and burned to the ground. Not wanting to rely on the fire department any more, Clark built another structure made almost entirely of the stone gathered from the seacoast.

It was known as the Kennebunkport Castle, a magnificent structure complete with a grand music room, regal guestrooms and a wealth of furnishings.

Before construction began, Clark moved the cemetery to another location in town despite protests from local townspeople.

Edward Clark died in 1910. His widow and daughter lived in the Castle for another two years before selling the property to Edwin Robertson. Robertson tore down the castle and built yet another summer home in 1913, now the Harbor Watch Inn, for the sum of 166,000 dollars.

Robertson died in the 1920s. His wife and family remained until the 1950s when they sold to another party who opened as a lodging establishment.

In 1996 the Inn was purchased by Peter and Kristyn Martin. Two other family members have minority stakes in the business as well.

Kristyn was my tour guide and history teacher, an energetic businesswoman with a take charge attitude.

Kristyn stated that before they purchased the property they were informed about the Inn's haunted reputation. They heard stories about how the wait staff would close down the dining room for the evening, pushing in the chairs and blowing out the

candles. Someone would often find one candle at a particular table relit and the chair ajar as if someone had just sat down.

They were also informed about a rocking chair in room #1, the old master bedroom. This chair had a habit of relocating itself, usually next to a window.

When the Martins purchased the Inn, Kristyn's nephew, an owner and contractor, began restoration work. At the end of the day he would always turn the heat down, only to come in the next day and find the heat turned up. This happened so frequently that he began to lecture the ghost about heating bills, politely asking it to leave the heat alone.

A local painter working in room #1 also reported finding the heat turned up on a daily basis.

Years ago a former owner employed a handyman to retile the Inn's bathrooms. I was informed the tiles were not very attractive. When the workers arrived one morning to begin tiling they discovered that all the tiles had been thrown down a flight of stairs. Apparently, the ghost did not approve of the tiles.

The next incident happened to Kristyn while she was working in her office, trying to organize things before their grand opening. She was completely alone on the second floor. While she was working the distant sound of music was heard emanating from the hallway. Upon investigation she realized it was coming from room #1. A bit frightened she called for her nephew who was downstairs. "Did you turn the radio on?" she asked.

"It wasn't me," he replied.

"Was anyone else up here?"

"Not to my knowledge." They both gingerly crept into the room and turned the radio off. Kristyn said they even checked the alarm, but there was no correlation.

The most shocking story to date came from an employee. One afternoon one of the Inn's waitresses was upstairs by herself. She had just departed the office, when suddenly she witnessed the ghostly figure of a woman standing in the doorway of room #1. She fled down the stairs as fast as she could and said, "That is the last time I go upstairs alone." She described the apparition as a short older woman with gray hair.

This same waitress mentioned her four-year-old niece while upstairs said that an old woman beckoned to her to come into room #1 and play the piano with her.

No one is certain who this entity is or what family she belongs to.

Kristyn stated that all of the encounters have been positive and their resident ghost is considered to be quite friendly. However, there's no denying the fact at the Harbor Watch Inn that someone has returned!

Harbor Watch Inn
Kennebunkport, Maine
207-967-3358

A Wedding Story

"When is she getting married? July what? Well, where in God's name is this place? Kennebunkport? Do you have any idea what the traffic will be like from Cape Cod in mid July! What do you mean I'm in the wedding! I have to rent a tuxedo?"

With a grimace on my face, I hastily packed up the car and traveled from Cape Cod to Kennebunkport to attend my sister's wedding. Not that I wasn't overjoyed for my sister, but weddings have always been a bit of a struggle for me.

The wedding was to be held at the Nonantum Resort, Kennebunkport, Maine. Not being familiar with the Inn, I decided to stay with my wife's family for the weekend, while my family resided at the Nonantum. I arrived at the Inn at six o'clock in the evening. The rehearsal dinner was about to commence. I took one look at the Inn and came to the realization I had made a grave mistake. "Do you want stay here?' my mother asked.

"I think I could be persuaded," I replied.

"I'm sorry," the night manager said, "we're completely booked." Of course, I had no one to blame but myself.

The Nonantum is one of the largest Inns in Kennebunkport and emphatically one of the loveliest. This four-story beauty is a blend of elegance and comfort. The main lobby is adorned with white wicker furniture, hand woven Orientals and gleaming hard wood floors. The baby grand piano and oversized fireplace seem to enrich the Inn's décor.

The Nonantum's sprawling grounds are joined in harmony with the majestic Kennebunkport River. This placid body of water is food for the soul, especially around sunset, as the river is illuminated with an iridescent glow.

The main dining room, with spectacular river views serves traditional favorites, using only the freshest of ingredients. The seafood is to die for.

If you have any questions or are in need of assistance, the Nonantum's courteous staff is always there to help. Every guest is treated with the utmost respect.

The Inn had its beginnings in July of 1884. At the time there were 28 rooms and a staff of ten people. Today, there are 117 rooms and approximately seventy-five employees.

After the rehearsal dinner I decided to pay a visit to some family members staying on the second floor. Walking down the long corridors alone, I thought to myself, this Inn has to have a ghost, it just has to. That very night I inquired at the front desk. "Does your Inn have a ghost?" I asked.

Tim, the night manager, replied, "I think you better ask Tina Hewett, General Manager, if it's okay to talk about this." Tina was very helpful, she told me a good place to start was housekeeping.

The head housekeeper and some of her staff members have witnessed some very strange occurrences over the years. Lights have been known to suddenly turn on for no apparent reason. Doors can frequently be heard slamming shut, when no one is around. Voices have even been heard emanating from empty rooms.

Another bizarre event that used to transpire involved furniture being moved, in particular couches and chairs found at the end of the hallways. In the past, while vacuuming the hallways, chambermaids have suddenly looked back and found the wicker couches and chairs repositioned. Stranger still, the furniture seemed to be facing them. "Its like the ghosts were relaxing and watching us work," said one of the staff members.

After the interview with housekeeping, I made my way to the front desk, where I briefly interviewed two more employees. I was told about a woman who complained after being kept awake all night by the person in the room next to hers. The woman said she constantly heard heavy breathing and loud coughing all night long. She was in a state of disbelief when she was informed by the desk clerk that the room next to hers was unoccupied.

I concluded my interviewing with Tim, the Night Manager. I'll let him tell you about his first ghostly encounter.

"The first incident that I recall was one evening in early autumn of 1990. Myself and another employee named Teresa were standing at the front desk. From where we stood we had a clear view of the front entrance to the hotel. The doors are of solid wood with glass panes and are fairly heavy. We heard the doorknob unlatch and in entered a young couple returning from dinner. They closed the door and we heard the door latch firmly as it was shut. They strolled across the lobby and got to where we were standing. We then heard the door latch again and instinctively looked in the direction of the door. The door swung open as if the let someone in and then slowly closed and latched itself again. There was no one there and Teresa and I just looked at each other."

Another incident occurred in the spring of 1994. The Inn employed a night watchman to monitor the main part of the Inn. It was early spring and the Inn was not open to guests. The electricity was shut off on the upper three floors and all guestroom doors were left ajar. While making his rounds the night watchman carried a large flashlight. As he patrolled the third floor the flashlight suddenly went out, followed by what he described as a deep moaning sound coming from the hallway above him. The unnerved security guard scampered down in the dark to the first floor. He said the incident gave him the creeps but didn't scare him enough to feel any danger.

In late October of 1995, Tim received a frantic phone call from a guest staying on the third floor. "Should we evacuate?" said the guest. "What do you mean?" said Tim. "Don't you feel that? My room, it's shaking." Tim dashed into the elevator and headed up to the third floor. When he arrived, the guest said the shaking had just stopped. Neither Tim nor any other guest felt this mysterious shaking.

Tim has heard noises, such as footsteps by the front desk, and he has witnessed a salad plate spin around in a complete circle by itself. Other employees have had similar experiences as well.

The Nonantum Resort
Kennebunkport, Maine
207-967-4050
800-552-5651

EMMA'S WATCHING

"Oh what a view." If it's a secluded Victorian mansion you've been searching for, look no further than the Tides Inn by-the-Sea. (Kennebunkport, Maine.) Set on majestic Goose Rocks beach this Victorian gem beckons with elegant simplicity. Sit back, relax, have a glass of Chardonnay on the lovely veranda. If you can tear yourself away from the magnificent views of the rocky coastline, I'll take you inside for a brief tour and then I will introduce you to the Innkeepers.

Casual elegance seems to be the theme. The spacious living room with its beautiful fieldstone fireplace seems to emanate a feeling of relaxation and comfort. Interesting antiques dot the Inn throughout and the twenty-two guestrooms are all uniquely decorated. Their restaurant, with its superb ocean views, serves sumptuous cuisine by romantic candlelight.

Marie Henriksen and daughter Kristin Blomberg purchased the Inn twenty-five years ago. Marie fell in love not only with the Inn but with the beautiful surroundings as well.

Kristin, a friendly and outgoing person, will make you feel right at home. In fact when you depart, you will honestly feel as if you have made a new friend.

From greeting the guests to refinishing their own hardwood floors, Marie and Kristin make a charming and unique mother-daughter team.

The Inn itself dates back to 1899. It was originally built by architect John Calvin Stevens and owned by a woman named Emma Foss. It was constructed for the sole purpose of being an Inn and at the time was known as the New Belvidere Inn. The Inn played host to may well known people including Teddy Roosevelt in 1900 and Sir Arthur Conan Doyle in 1904. The original guest book with these famous signatures is on display for the guest's enjoyment.

Now, I suppose you want to hear about the Inn's resident ghost, Emma Foss. As mentioned earlier, Emma was the original founder and it's her presence that is thought to still linger throughout the Inn.

Kristin stated that as soon as her mother purchased the Inn back in 1972 they immediately sensed a presence. The fire alarm outside room 25 (Emma's room) would frequently go off in the middle of the night for no apparent reason. It had become such a nuisance the alarm sensor had to be moved.

As time went on, stranger and more intriguing events began to transpire. Reports of beds shaking and guests feeling as if someone was actually tucking them into bed at night began to surface.

Kristin spoke of a gentleman staying in room 29. She said he checked out very early in the morning. The next night Kristin received a startling phone call. It was the man that had checked out of room 29 the previous day. He said "I was lying in bed and began to sense someone was watching me. As soon as I opened my eyes I found an apparition of a stern looking woman staring down upon me. I then jumped out of bed and tried swiping at the ghost. At that point the apparition suddenly vanished."

Another sighting was reported in room 29 by two painters. The men were in the middle of painting a dresser when they discovered they were not alone. An apparition of a middle-aged woman wearing a blue and white-stripped dress appeared to be leaning against the door jam, watching their every move. The painters were so moved by this experience, they painted a beautiful mural with Emma's picture on it. The mural can be viewed on the wall beside the staircase going up to the second floor.

Kristin recalls a time when a guest she describes as being very uptight was residing in room 11. One morning, he came down in a huff and asked if there had been an earthquake the night before. Kristin said no and asked why. The man then proceeded to tell her that while he was sitting on the toilet, it started to shake. At that point, Kristin said she almost lost it. She began laughing, which just angered him further. "Maybe it was the ghost," said Kristin.

"I don't believe in ghosts," the man replied. He then turned on the weather channel to see if there was any news about an earthquake.

Kristin feels Emma has a problem with some men, particularly men that are uptight. Apparently years ago when Emma owned the Inn, she was eventually forced to sell it to her desk clerk, Mr. Allen. Kristin believes there was bad blood between them, which brings us to our final story.

A gentleman from Massachusetts, who was described as having an easygoing personality, was staying in room 9. He came down one morning and said he felt as if someone had beaten him up in the middle of the night. He said he actually had multiple bruises on his legs. Kristin was in a state of disbelief. She thought if it was Emma, why would she harm a man who was such a nice person. Then it dawned on her. As previously mentioned, there was reportedly bad blood between Emma and her desk clerk, Mr. Allen. Now, I'll give you three guesses as to what the first name of the gentleman staying in room number 9 was.

The Tides Inn By-The-Sea
Kennebunkport, Maine
207-967-3757

The End 161

Haunted Inns of New England

Other Books from On Cape Publications

Haunted Cape Cod & the Islands
by Mark Jasper
$14.95

Howie Schneider Unshucked:
A Cartoon Collection about the Cape, the Country and Life Itself
by Howie Schneider
$11.95

Quabbin:
A History & Explorer's Guide
by Michael Tougias
$18.95

Baseball by the Beach:
A History of America's National Pastime on Cape Cod
by Christopher Price
$14.95

In the Footsteps of Thoreau:
25 Historic & Nature Walks on Cape Cod
by Adam Gamble
$14.95

Cape Cod
by Henry David Thoreau (Audio)
$19.95

Walking the Shores of Cape Cod
by Elliott Carr
$14.95

Cape Cod, Martha's Vineyard & Nantucket, the Geologic Story
by Robert N. Oldale
$14.95

1880 Atlas of Barnstable County:
Cape Cod's Earliest Atlas
$39.95

Sea Stories of Cape Cod and the Islands
by Admont G. Clark
$39.95

www.oncapepublications.com